About Bliss

of related interest

To My Trans Sisters
Charlie Craggs
ISBN 978 1 78592 343 2
eISBN 978 1 78450 668 1

My Child Told Me They're Trans... What Do I Do?
A Q&A Guide for Parents of Trans Children
Edited by Brynn Tannehill
ISBN 978 1 83997 277 5
eISBN 978 1 83997 278 2

He's Always Been My Son
A Mother's Story about Raising Her Transgender Son
Janna Barkin
ISBN 978 1 78592 747 8
eISBN 978 1 78450 525 7

Fighting for My Trans Son's Life, Joy, and Fertility

Cristina Olivetti

Foreword by Diane Ehrensaft

Jessica Kingsley Publishers
London and Philadelphia

First published in Great Britain in 2025 by Jessica Kingsley Publishers
An imprint of John Murray Press

1

Content Warning: This book mentions transphobia and suicide.

A CIP catalogue record for this title is available from the British Library and the Library of Congress

ISBN 978 1 80501 039 5
eISBN 978 1 80501 040 1

Printed and bound in the United States by Integrated Books International

Jessica Kingsley Publishers' policy is to use papers that are natural, renewable and recyclable products and made from wood grown in sustainable forests. The logging and manufacturing processes are expected to conform to the environmental regulations of the country of origin.

Jessica Kingsley Publishers
Carmelite House
50 Victoria Embankment
London EC4Y 0DZ

www.jkp.com

John Murray Press
Part of Hodder & Stoughton Ltd
An Hachette Company

The authorised representative in the EEA is Hachette Ireland,
8 Castlecourt Centre, Dublin 15, D15 XTP3, Ireland (email: info@hbgi.ie)

Contents

To my husband and children,
Thank you for sharing a life worth writing about.

Author's Note

Parents of gender nonconforming children are overseeing a cultural sea change in gender. We are required to make high stakes decisions impacting our children's long-term social, emotional, and physical health while learning a new model of gender that shakes the foundations of what we thought we knew about life and about ourselves. During a time when social scientists, biologists, health practitioners, and transgender individuals learn something new about gender diversity almost daily, even the most supportive parents struggle to keep up with current information and best practices.

At the same time, we have had no choice but to confront the volatile political backlash that is currently occurring against transgender rights. Many of us, myself included, have become accidental political activists. In the few years it has taken to write and publish our family's story, more states than ever before have filed and passed legislation to restrict the lives of trans people. To give a sense, by the end of 2020, which is where the book you are about to read concludes, 60 state-level anti-trans bills had been filed. At the end of 2021 that number increased to 132, and at the end of 2022, anti-trans bills introduced at the state level numbered 155 or more.* In 2021 Arkansas became the first state in the nation to ban access to gender-affirming care for minors, and since then Tennessee, Arizona, and Alabama have followed suit. Numerous other laws restricting access to sports, locker rooms and bathrooms, preventing people from changing state-issued identity documents to align with their affirmed gender, and banning insurance coverage for trans healthcare have been filed and passed. At the same time, states like California, Oregon, Washington, New York, Massachusetts, and others have strengthened their protections for the trans community, guaranteeing insurance coverage, providing safe harbor, and offering the trans community the kind of legal support necessary to live what most people would consider a "normal" American life.

Looking back, it seems to me that our family grappled with the issue of my son's gender at a flash in history that encouraged us to think proactively and ambitiously on his behalf. We had the mental space to think creatively about what could be possible for his future, rather than worry over how we would keep him safe in an increasingly hostile environment. To be sure, the threat of hostility loomed, and yet, we lucked into a historical and geographical context that supported our bold hopes. For parents reading this book, my hope is that our story will give you both respite and inspiration. Professionals across the board—psychologists and psychiatrists, pediatricians and endocrinologists, educators and social workers—have come to the unanimous conclusion that gender is wildly more complex than the binary model my generation and generations before us understood. If your child is presenting a different gender than the one they were assigned at birth, they

* https://translegislation.com

are going to be okay. No, more than okay. Your child is unique, perhaps even gifted. Many, perhaps most, of the difficulties you and your family will face have everything to do with American culture wars and very little to do with the child you love so deeply.

In the current context there were many reasons, most especially to do with my son's privacy and his safety, for me not to share my family's story with the world. But my son has made clear for many years now that raising public awareness about gender identity is important to him. He has believed in this book from the beginning. And although he is a minor and his thoughts on many things are likely to change, my sense is that his commitment to helping others in his community is one that will stay with him throughout his lifetime.

He and I are both aware that our family has lived in a fortunate context when it comes to gender diversity. We live in the San Francisco Bay Area, we have stable finances and excellent health insurance, and because of my work as a writer, we have had easier access to trans writers and their stories. Because of these factors, my son is safer and has more robust support than other trans kids his age. As a family our collective imagination has been freer to envision a bright and generative future. Especially in the face of the current political backlash, it feels important to speak out from our vantage point to celebrate gender diversity and normalize the expectation that our trans and nonbinary citizens will live bold, proud lives, with full access to their potential and their human rights.

I wrote this book to organize my own thinking during the year before my husband and I made some of the most long-lasting health decisions on my trans son's behalf. I had already been in the habit of writing to my three children for many years. With the birth of each one I purchased a beige hardcover notebook in which I jotted down notes to them from time to time. The stack of three has lived on my nightstand or near it for as long as I have been a parent. Some years I recorded many observations and some years I hardly wrote a word. But as the reality of my son's life became clearer to me, it felt natural to consider the many aspects of our experience within the container of a habit I had already established.

When I decided to share our journey, I thought I would be writing in traditional narrative form, but I ran into a problem of language that every transgender person knows intimately. The assignment of gendered pronouns tends to obscure transgender children's identity. For years trans children are referred to in words that do not reflect who they are inside, and the current convention is that once a person's correct gender has been affirmed, they will be referred to using the name and set of pronouns that aligns with their identity even when telling stories about the past. For many trans people, using the name or pronouns that were assigned to them before their correct gender identity was affirmed is painful. "Deadnaming" is one word used to describe the harsh discomfort of using these old names. When I tell stories about my son in spoken language, the current convention works imperfectly but well enough.

But when I began writing down stories about my son's childhood, it interfered with accurately immersing you, the reader, in the relationship I had with him during his early years, which, in its essence, transcended the language we had at our disposal. I decided to tell our story in the epistolary form using the second person in reference to my son, because it renders our relationship with much higher fidelity than other pronoun conventions allow.

I'm offering the most visceral representation of my relationship with my son that I felt I could create.

These letters make deep sense in another way, too. Ultimately, this book is for my son. My hope is that through an honest and thoughtful documentation of our journey together, he will know his foundation with all its cracks and weaknesses so that he can build a sturdy adult life characterized by wholeness. I am humbled by the fact that many of my parenting decisions, including the one to write this book, have been a leap of faith. And like all parents, I hope that on the whole I have done right by my child. May love always guide us as we labor on behalf of a future we will never know.

Whatever errors in perception or in fact that appear in the story you are about to read are wholly my own. For the protection of minors especially, identifying details of some individuals have been changed.

Foreword

Diane Ehrensaft

I write this Foreword to *About Bliss* at a time when folks like me, pediatric gender-affirmative practitioners, find themselves dubbed both angels and devils. I write on the heels of a California Republican Party meeting in San Francisco to address "trans" issues, in a state that declares itself the sanctuary state for trans people. Cristina Olivetti, the author of this book and mother of a trans youth, reveals how afraid she feels in the face of the legislative attacks on trans children and their families, even while living in a state that strongly supports transgender rights. To her transgender son she writes, "Sometimes I feel like I've handed you a daisy for a gunfight." What she has handed him, and us, is the poignant story of a mother willing to share thoughts, feelings, actions, and her own education as she walks alongside her child in his gender journey. There could be no better weapon to slay gender dragons.

Presently, it is the best of times and the worst of times for transgender youth and their families in our country. On the one hand, led by the children, their families, the trans community, and the providers serving them, a new world has emerged in which genders in all their variations are celebrated and pathways are carved for children to be the gender they are, rather than the one others think they ought to be. On the other hand, some people, out of fear, confusion, or political opportunism, want to shut down those pathways and stop our gender-creative children from going forward. It is in this climate that Cristina's voice rings out so clearly and eloquently, reminding us of the beauty of the gender journey, for both parent and child. Although most families encounter a few challenges along the way, it is a legitimate path toward human wholeness. But if you think about it, what is a rose without its thorns?

I have had the privilege of meeting thousands of transgender, nonbinary, and gender-diverse youth in my role as Director of Mental Health at the University of California Child & Adolescent Gender Center. We are an interdisciplinary team of gender specialists tasked with joining youth and their families to co-create a gender health plan that will facilitate each youth living authentically in their gender, surrounded by acceptance and protected from aspersion. Some of the younger youth will receive puberty blockers as part of that plan, an intervention that puts puberty on hold and wards off an unwanted endogenous puberty if it is discordant with the youth's affirmed gender identity. Some of the youth, when ready, will choose gender-affirming hormones to align their bodies with the gender they know themselves to be.

For youth seeking medical gender care, both puberty blockers and hormone therapy will affect that youth's fertility by suppressing the growth and development of reproductive cells. This impediment to future fertility is a significant thorn for youth and their parents to manage. For those of us who are pediatric gender care providers, we find ourselves in uncharted territory. Gender-affirmative care disrupts the guidance that we typically offer to teenagers in our culture, in which we encourage youth to use protection and not even think about having a baby until much, much later. But in the case of gender-creative youth, we now need to encourage teenagers to think about just the opposite—how they might or might not want to have a baby. And we need them to think about it now, not some day in the distant future. Typically, this is the last thing on a young gender-diverse teen's mind when they come to our clinic.

For gender-creative youth, access to puberty blockers and gender-affirming options is not just a choice among many choices, but a potential life saver. And often, youth experience the desire to move forward toward consolidating their gender with life-and-death urgency. Asking an anxious teen to be reflective about their future family-building when they feel so urgent about living their life *now* is one of the most challenging parts of being a gender-creative parent.

But often it is a burning question for that teen's parents, who are old enough and mature enough to take a long view of life and who are charged with the responsibility of making informed decisions on their child's behalf. Successfully navigating this emotional, high-stakes family negotiation is the territory that gender-affirmative practitioners, gender-creative youth, and the parents of those youth are just beginning to chart.

About Bliss will take you into the deepest crevices and alleyways of one family's excursions toward gender euphoria for their child, with fertility as a highlighted aspect of that journey. Cristina invites us into the inner world of a mother doing her best to raise her son to be his true gender self. Alongside her son she learns that gender transition is a process, and that a teenager's thoughts and feelings about themselves and about their future evolve over the course of this personal transformation. Burdened by the urgency of avoiding a puberty that is not right for them, trans youth will often say that they are willing to sacrifice their future fertility to live authentically. But as you will see in Jake's poignant story, these initial responses are only the start, and not the end, of the conversation.

For those readers who are themselves parents of a gender-diverse child, of whatever age, you may have noticed the absence of a standardized guidebook for raising a gender fabulous person, especially when it comes to having conversations about saving eggs or sperm for the future. Cristina is a warm and thoughtful companion for you on this journey. Through the letters she writes to Jake the year before Jake starts hormone therapy you will bear witness to Cristina's close consideration of her son's future as a potential parent, her thoughtful observation of her son's development, and their co-created solution to preserving Jake's reproductive choices for the future.

Transgender youth and the transgender community are accomplishing an enormous feat of the human spirit. Being trans is a real thing. If we give trans youth the support they need when they experience gender dysphoria, we will bear witness to a kind of flourishing that I would call gender euphoria.

Letter 1
March 2019: The Point of No Return

Dear Jake,

When Dr. Zee looked at your chart and said, "Wow, you're almost 13—about to be a real teenager," she was very matter of fact, her delivery as straight as her smooth black hair and the dress pants she wore. Right after that she announced that you would start your testosterone shots in a year, when you were 14. "I like to have my patients start puberty before the beginning of ninth grade," is how she put it, "because the transition into high school is a big change for all kids." Your eyes lit up; this is what you have been waiting for, your first step into biological masculinity. And yet, I heard myself asking her if we could wait a little bit longer. I don't know why exactly, except that more time is the one thing I keep wishing for. And as if she could read my thoughts, she asked, "Is there a reason to want more time?"

In the fluorescent light of the exam room, with the white paper crackling beneath your thighs, and the cabinet full of syringes staring us down, there was no reason I could put easily into words. I loved you as a boy, it was not that. My story as your mom does not include grief over losing the child I thought I had. You have been yourself for as long as I can remember.

But when the doctor asked whether there was a reason to want more time, the image that flickered through my awareness was of your first testosterone shot. The barrel of the syringe marked like a ruler with its black tick marks and a bead of oily liquid glimmering at the tip like an opal. Now that we are in the last 12 months before you start testosterone, I find that this picture pops into my head more often, especially when it's bedtime and you ask me for "just one more minute" of back scratching, as if the shot itself marks the end of your childhood and the beginning of you belonging to the wider world, with its medicalized pathways, its general disregard for gender-diverse people, and all the quick public cruelty that characterizes so much of public discourse these days.

I hope that when the time comes for that shot, I feel more at peace than I do now. Every family raising a gender-diverse child in this era of flux manages fear and uncertainty. Some families fear for their child's safety; others fear their child will be rejected by their school or their peers or other family members. Still others fear that their children are falling prey to an internet trend they do not understand and that might not even be real. The specific concerns are as unique as each family on this journey. Our fears reveal the values we hold most dear, the values we are most afraid to revise. The process we are overseeing as parents is entirely different from what we understood growing up. And this is all made more complicated by the fact that the technology for aligning your body with your inner experience during puberty is still relatively new. The first American pediatric gender clinic opened in 2009 in Boston, which means that the first cohort of kids to go through this process are only now entering their twenties. They are adults, but just barely.

In our family, Dad and I initially grappled most with whether a gender identity merited biological treatment. We both came of age when American feminists were leading the culture in understanding that gender is a social construct. Being a Women's Studies major, I was trained to not only believe but also to build arguments around the idea that masculinity and femininity were collections of roles and expectations, and that they had nothing to do with biology and everything to do with cultural expectations. So, when you started to be drawn towards clothes and activities that boys usually preferred, we did not think twice about it. It wasn't until you started seeming nervous about the ways your body would change during puberty that we started to consider that we might have to revise our position.

I can still remember our first trip to the pediatric gender clinic like it was yesterday. You were 11. In my mind's eye I can still see the slick plated glass of the recently built hospital; I can smell the fumes of the brand-new elevator; and I can feel the pop of cheer that rose up in me when I first saw the huge orange penguins stenciled onto the walls of your exam room. The bubble of instant cheer popped quickly in the face of my anxiety. After all, those bright orange birds were one more reminder that you were just a kid. The first doctor to join us in the exam room tried so hard to put us at ease. He entered wearing a simple beige sweater that hugged his shoulders. No white coat, just plain clothes, and why should I remember this, but polka dot socks.

So much about that day shocked me. From how the doctor spoke about gender to the specifics of the medical treatment that was recommended for you. It all felt predicated on the idea that there were two possible identities, one for kids who liked short hair and rough-and-tumble play, and another for kids who liked glitter and dresses. When I asked how they handled genders that were not purely "all-boy" or "all-girl," the doctor paused as if to puzzle over the idea, and then said, "We don't offer a blended option." It felt like we were being sold a Tesla that was also a time-machine, programmed to return us to the days when boys were boys and girls were girls, and the new technology could clean up all the messy gender fluidity that your generation has been showing us.

The only exchange that made sense to me that day was between you and Dr. Henderson, the psychologist we saw during our visit. She asked, "How do you feel about growing up? Is that something you can imagine doing?" And without missing a beat you responded, "No way." Definitively—feet firmly planted, eyes wide and emphatic, a lift in your chin and voice, as if she must have been kidding, as if you were shocked that someone might assume growing up with all its fleshy changes and the accompanying public display of maleness or femaleness was an easy prospect for you to think about.

Your absolute inability to imagine your future struck me like a tectonic force. The muscles and bones between my shoulder blades kicked back as if they had taken a hard blow. And I realized for the first time that none of us—not you, not me, not Dad—none of us knew how you, with your short blonde hair and black sneakers and sports shorts, you who were called "sir" or "buddy" or "young man" by every waiter or flight attendant we ever met, you, whose body was about to be pushed over the falls in a cascade of estrogen—none of us knew how you were going to grow up. When I heard you declare in one short phrase, "No way," the fault lines of our lives heaved.

Shortly after that first visit, you started taking hormone blockers.

The blockers have paused puberty's progress, and if you stopped taking them your endogenous puberty would proceed unchanged. Beginning testosterone, on the other hand, will cause permanent changes to your body. You will grow the shoulders you have so often imagined having. Your vocal cords will thicken and cause your voice to lower. You'll get facial hair, and maybe even end up with my own father's baldness. And along with all this, is the possible side effect that you will be infertile. Before we started this process, I knew that people could be transgender and that living in a transgender body was complicated, but I never imagined that to live your life authentically you would have to give up your fertility. And certainly, Dad and I had never considered what it would mean for us to steward you through that decision while you were still a minor and we served as your legal guardians.

Once, when your older sister was ten, she came back from a camping trip with a tick lodged in the skin of her underarm. It had swelled to the size of a raisin, its head burrowed into her flesh, a thin collar of gray where the bug started to disappear beneath her skin. I got the tweezers and pulled at it as gently as I could, but I blew it. The body came off and the rest of it remained buried, so I had to call the doctor. She asked us to stop by her office so she could look at it. It wasn't terrible, she said, but it wasn't great either, so she prescribed a round of antibiotics.

When your sister swallowed that pink liquid, I was struck by the finality of it, the fact that there was no going back in time. The tick had bitten her, the medicine was swallowed; whatever the world had been before the camping trip, it was no more. It was an overblown response to a common bump in the road of childhood, and yet the kernel of thought it produced felt durable and true. We had come to an absolute fork in the timeline of her life, a fork that bent farther away from its origin when she swallowed the medicine. Had I checked the bottle? Had the pharmacist dosed the right prescription? What if there had been some terrible mistake, a failure of packaging at the factory, or a contaminated ingredient? I thought of the long chain of details that needed to be executed correctly—the conveyor belts and packing machines, the delivery trucks, the hands of factory workers and pharmacists, the judgment of her pediatrician, and, of course, my delivering the proper dose with my own hands. I understood your sister's safety depended on so many small things going right. By the time she swallowed the liquid what was done was done. The future was locked and sealed, a course set, and we could only hope we had gotten it right.

Your sister healed just fine. But the insight about the way things could go wrong (including my own human fallibility) stuck. Until that day, I believed that the future could always be mended the way torn fabric could be sewn back together: maybe not perfectly, but good enough to live with. Tires could be patched. Panes of glass could be replaced. Hard work would inevitably be rewarded. Human intelligence could prevail in problems of medicine and technology. Until that day I felt life was within my grasp. But after your sister Alison took that one dose of medicine, I realized that no amount of hard work, prayer, or faith could undo what had been done. The swift current of your sister's life swept us past blurry shorelines and revealed how little control we really had. A wave of nausea rolled through my gut as my body absorbed the truth of our vulnerability.

I have started writing to you more frequently this year, because I have not yet accepted that the choice is as binary as it has been presented to you. Whenever I drive through the heart of Silicon Valley, the blinding sun reflecting off all those glass buildings like a river of light, I cannot stop thinking that a better solution is just around the corner.

But we cannot put off that first dose of testosterone forever, and an ending, that fork in the road, is now in sight. Your body has been hovering in a rare and fluid in-between-ness, but when you start testosterone, we—you and Dad and me—will have made the best choices we can. Another way of saying this is that you will, after a brief pause to consider what's right for you, finally see your way through to growing up.

Dad and I have had to make decisions on your behalf (just like we have for your sisters), but in your case, with your gender, we have been making our decisions with imperfect information, imperfect technology, in the context of an imperfect and often unkind culture. We have done our best to engage with you eye-to-eye about your adult self. How does he look? What kind of family does he want to have? How does he want to be seen? What does he need to be safe? As we face the date that you will start testosterone, all of our usual strategies—research, conversations with you, meetings with experts—feel thin.

One of the only thoughts that comforts me lately is a vision of you that came to me a few years ago. It was in the middle of one of our hardest times. I was falling asleep. In the liquid slip before going dark I was visited by a vision of you. You were about 30 and I saw you standing next to my bed. I knew I was near dying—it was a death bed scene of all things—and I watched it unfold from afar as if it were happening to someone else. You were tall. Your shoulders stooped a little in your button-down shirt. Next to you stood a child, a boy, maybe three years old, holding your hand. I looked up at you and struggled to speak.

"Look at what you've accomplished," I said to you in the dream, "Just look..."

This vision came as a comfort to me, because I knew then that you would make it. Not only would you make it, but you would also live a life we have often been told is not possible. There is no real reason to believe in a vision like this. There are no facts to back it up, no research I've seen yet that would support my imagination. But that has not mattered a whit to me. What has mattered has been the wholeness I sensed in you at that moment. Adulthood was going to be good for you. We would figure out this business of growing up, and the future would fill itself in.

Looking back, I probably should have been more curious about the me dying part. It seems absurd to have bypassed the centrality of my own mortality in this scene that I return to so often. But here's the thing: the possibility of a child's long-term future requires the parent to accept the fact of their own finitude. And from the moment your sister, red and hot and wriggling, rested atop my incised, post C-section belly, this knowledge has been retained inside me. Like the taproot of an old oak, it became a hidden cord tying me to an ever-present truth so nonnegotiable it's not worth thinking about.

Day-in, day-out I pack lunches. I drive my white minivan up and down the El Camino. I schedule doctors' appointments and playdates and babysitters and carpools. I write a few pages before cutting apples for snacks then putting the pot of water on the stove to start dinner. Meanwhile, my body telegraphs the wordless offering of mothers everywhere: here is my flesh for your wholeness.

REFLECTION QUESTIONS

- How are you feeling about your child's gender? What fears, if any, do you have?
- What kind of information would ease your fears? What topics might you want to explore with your doctor at your first gender clinic visit to feel safer and more grounded?
- Can you identify which deeply held personal values (for example, many parents value keeping their child healthy and safe) seem threatened or at risk for you when you consider your child's identity? If so, what are they? What perspectives might you need to revise? Who do you trust to be a productive and ongoing thought partner to talk about big topics like this? If you anticipate a change in perspective will seriously impact your current life, who might support you in thinking through these changes? How can you foster an ongoing connection with this person?
- What do you need to know about hormone blockers? What do you want to ask about potential surgeries? Who can the doctor connect you with to help sort out your child's questions about gender identity from other mental health concerns you might have? Are there professionals your doctor might know—therapists, parenting coaches, gender support group leaders—that your doctor might help you contact? What resources could you request to support your own journey to understand gender diversity?

Letter 2

April 2019: The Beginnings of Your Boyishness

When you were getting ready for your friend Adam's Bar Mitzvah the other night, I couldn't help but remember the beginnings of your boyishness. The first time I recalled you wearing a blazer (which you called your "tuxedo") was for a holiday concert in elementary school a few months after you had cut your hair short. The big question you had that night was whether your choir director would be mad at you for wearing boys' clothes. I promised you that if you wore something formal, I didn't think she would mind.

The night of the concert I received so many texts from parents and teachers (the choir director among them) cheering you on, thrilled by your zest. Few of them would have dared to cross gender norms when they were young the way you did. We were all proud of you, and proud of the environment we had created in which you felt free to be yourself. How I loved the black blazer you wore that night, and the red velvet jacket you wore the next holiday season, and then the black vest, the green vest, and the many navy-blue blazers that have accumulated in your closet like a small army.

Your boyishness had even earlier beginnings than that holiday concert, though. There was the fall when you were four years old and Alison was six, and I took you to the children's shoe store in the mall to buy back-to-school shoes. It was a warm end-of-summer day. The hills behind Stanford had turned deep gold, and red twiggy roses climbed the fence that marked the edge of campus. The shopping center was packed with moms and school-aged kids running the same set of errands we were. In the shoe store, patent leather Mary Janes, purple flats, and hot, pink lace-ups were displayed in rows. On an island in the middle, dark shoes, mostly sneakers, along with loafers and mini lace-up Oxfords, formed concentric circles. While Alison picked out a few different Mary Janes to try out, you circled the center island. You didn't let yourself look right at the shoes, you just side-eyed them while you held your arms stick straight by your sides, as if you were resisting temptation. I asked you if you saw anything you liked. You shrugged your shoulders. "Girls' shoes are boring," you said. That summer, everything you did not like had become "boring." Polly Pockets were boring. American Girl dolls were boring. Broccoli was boring.

I asked you which shoes looked interesting to you, and you pointed to a pair of sneakers on the center island. I smiled. I liked your preference for the boys' shoes. It was more evidence that I had raised you and your sisters to believe you had choices, and by proxy that I had choices too, even though I had decided to stop working in high tech and sometimes felt otherwise. I had ambivalent feelings about leaving my career, but Dad made a lot more money than I did, and I knew that the combination of two full-time jobs in Silicon Valley and three kids was more than our system could handle. The notion of choice was important to me, because choice meant agency. When the gray-haired sales clerk returned from the stockroom with Alison's shoes and saw you circling the center island, he scolded you. "Little Miss, those are the boys' shoes," he said.

You looked at me. I told you it was okay to try on the boys' sneakers. When you raised your eyebrows in a way that asked, Are you sure, Mom?, I told you, shoes are shoes.

Given permission you knew exactly what you wanted. You pointed at a pair of black sneakers with orange flames along the sides. Red lights set the flames on fire when the soles of the shoes tapped the ground. The clerk returned with your size. You watched closely as he unfolded the white tissue paper and then shimmied the shoes onto your feet. Once they were on you raced around the store jumping and stomping. I had to do a double take because as you ran in circles it looked like you had grown at least two inches from sheer joy. The clerk rang up the empty box. When we left you hopped two feet first across the threshold of the store.

That same year we were driving along Page Mill Road and you called out to me from the third row of the van. "Mom," you shouted, "when I grow up, I want to look like that guy." I looked out the window and there was a bare-chested white man in black jogging shorts. My first thought was—What on earth?

"That jogger?" I asked. He was running along the shoulder of the road. His pecks winked as he ran, and each of his stomach muscles was a perfect band around his middle. My second thought—Ironman. He was that cut.

"You mean you want six pack abs?" I asked. We had not cut your hair short yet. I can still see the blonde swooping underneath your chin.

"Yeah, I guess," you replied as you watched him recede in the distance.

I told you I thought he was too skinny. I did not want you or your sisters to have eating disorders. I explained that to get six pack abs you had to have a low body fat percentage. And then, to nip things in the bud, I made it clear that I did not want anyone in our family to have six pack abs. You didn't say anything else. I was thinking forward into anorexia. You were imagining the rest of your life. These days, when I think back on the two of us in the car, I am certain that I read this situation incorrectly.

Recently I asked you if you remembered this moment. You did. I asked you if you thought of yourself as a boy back then.

"I don't think so," you said. Then you paused to think for a minute, "I knew who I was. But I didn't use the word 'boy.'"

Seeing that shirtless jogger was a small moment. He should have been a forgettable scrap of memory, excised for efficiency's sake, but he has stuck around all these years. Neither one of us ever forgot the impression he made. Lately, I feel more and more compelled to record the small moments that linger in my awareness this way. We have no way of knowing what we don't know, and I want you to have any fragments I can figure out how to record that might turn out to be significant. Because our view of things changes; time obscures some things and clarifies others.

There were so many times that year, when your hair was still long, that you expressed your masculine self with joy: the day the firefighters visited school and you got to spray the hose across the parking lot, the afternoon you dressed like a pirate and pulled your little sister in a wooden boat around the kitchen, the weeks and weeks you picked out clothes that made you look more and more like a mini version of your father.

The joy I witnessed in you and felt when I was around you was the primary reason I resisted the term "gender dysphoria" at first. The diagnosis had come up when you were having trouble sleeping through the night (something I regarded as a typical childhood difficulty). I consulted with a couple of child psychologists. They took in your short hair and your tomboy clothes and hypothesized, rightly it turned out, that you were exploring your gender identity. But I didn't see what they saw. I saw a kid who was happy in jeans, who loved rough-and-tumble play, who wanted to fight fires when they grew up. To my mind, none of those ideas conflicted with having female body parts. Distress concerning one's gender was a defining feature of gender dysphoria, and what I perceived was far from distress. I saw bliss—the kind I associated with the everyday sensory joys of childhood. When gender dysphoria was suggested to me, the term hung in my ear like the opening line of a tragedy, a cosmic accident that I had somehow missed noticing.

If I had known that bliss and harmony were aspects of gender identity, I might have considered the diagnosis more seriously. But as it was, I did not want to pathologize a part of you that seemed to create so much confidence and happiness. And when I look back on your early years, I am almost always happy that we did not put you in months or years of gender therapy. You grew up in an environment that celebrated your gender expression (even though we didn't understand the full meaning of it when you were very young).

But there were costs. I failed to see the hurdles gender would cause as you got older, and when you experienced them we were unprepared. And there was the added fear after you took a boy's name after all—that for the rest of your life your childhood history would be one that could catch other people by surprise. If you had taken a boy's name and masculine pronouns earlier, I wondered whether that history would feel less threatening, less like something that could pop out at any time and create trouble, maybe even violence. The potential eruption of violence is a problem that almost all trans people face. Cis people make assumptions about other people's gender history and bodily history all the time. And occasionally I fantasize that we could have gotten ahead of it. If fewer people had known your incorrectly assigned gender, if we owned fewer family photographs or had fewer family memories during the years when we used the name and pronouns that were assigned to you at birth, maybe there would be less opportunity for accidental disclosure. We'll never know.

The night of Adam's Bar Mitzvah, you threw on a collared shirt, a black blazer, jeans, and sneakers with a red swoosh. You carefully combed your blonde hair so that it laid smooth across the top of your head. Like always, you worried about how you looked, and I assured you that you looked handsome. Like always you complained that I have to say that because I am your mother, which, though true, does not change the fact that you are handsome. Since you moved schools last year, in part so you could try out having a boy's name and pronouns, the group of people you were about to see at Adam's party did not know your gender history. You were just a guy named Jake, and your formal wear was unremarkable to them. There were no more anxious questions about whether anyone would disapprove of your clothes, and when we arrived there were no excited texts from parents. But to me there was still a thrill in seeing you dapper, with your hair combed and wearing your blazer with its squared-off shoulders. When the DJ announced it was time for the mother–son dance and we both turned to find one another, my insides blazed with a fierce joy.

We danced together, melting into the crowd of all the other mothers and sons, unnoticeable, the hugeness of our moment invisible to anyone but us. I teared up when you spun me under your arm, thinking to myself, "I have a son. I really have a son." Our dance amplified the feeling I always had whenever I'd been able to cut through the layers of thinking that short-circuit my experience of your gender—all those complicated questions about what it meant to you, about what it meant to me, of how it was read by others, of what it would mean to your future. In the moment, dancing, heart to heart, head to head, hand to hand, our mutual recognition transcended the coarseness of language. Our connection was and always will be a particular kind of bliss for me.

REFLECTION QUESTIONS

- Recall a moment when you have witnessed your child experience real joy. What was your child doing? What kinds of movements/sounds/gestures were they making that signaled their happiness? What does it feel like to recall this memory? Can you identify sensations in your own body that accompany your child's joy? How could your experience of your child's joy serve as a guide for you?
- Recall a moment when your child has been totally relaxed and at ease. What was your child doing? What were they wearing? Where were they? Were they alone or were they with a sibling, a friend, or a beloved pet? What do you feel like recalling your child's peace? Witnessing your child's peace, how does your own body feel? How could this sensation serve as a guide for you?

- If you have ever been able to take your child swimming in public, what was that like? Recall the most recent trip you made. How did it go? What did your child wear? How comfortable or uncomfortable were they? How did they feel about the activity? Public swimming is a context that evokes very strong feelings for children with gender dysphoria. If you think back to your last time taking your child swimming in a public place, what comes up for you? What might this moment be teaching you?
- Gender dysphoria is an experience of dysregulation that arises from the experience of having one's body read and seen by other people in a way that is very different than the person experiences themselves on the inside. People who do not experience gender dysphoria have a difficult time understanding this experience. However, if a person who normally experiences gender dysphoria gets even a small taste of gender alignment—for example when my son was allowed to choose boys' sneakers—their energy can suddenly shift in a positive way. Have you seen a moment like this happen for your child? How would you describe it? When did it happen? Can you identify what contributed to your child's experience of joy and freedom? Some people refer to this feeling as "gender euphoria." What specific elements do you think contribute to gender euphoria for your child?

Interview
Dr. Shawn Giammattei on Gender Dysphoria

Shawn Giammattei, PhD, is a clinical family psychologist and gender therapist. He is the founder of the TransFamily Alliance,* the Gender Health Training Institute,† and Quest Family Therapy.‡ He is a faculty member at the California School of Professional Psychology at Alliant International University. Shawn identifies as a queer male with a transgender history. His mission, through his private practice and various teaching positions, is to bring healing, knowledge, and real solutions to the problems affecting the trans community and their families.

Cristina: I wanted to start by asking you about gender dysphoria. Can you tell us a little bit about how this diagnosis came about? And how you think it supports the trans community, but is also a little confusing? What are the complexities with the tool?

Shawn: Well, in 1973, when homosexuality was eliminated from

* www.transfamilyalliance.com
† www.genderhealthtraining.com
‡ www.questfamilytherapy.com

the DSM* as a mental illness, gender identity disorder was introduced. It was a diagnosis that applied to anybody who was gender nonconforming. The problem with the DSM is that it is a collection of pathologies. It is a language that clinicians use to describe constellations of symptoms. But it's also very political. There is a lot in the DSM that's not based on science or data. It's just some guys got together and said, "Oh, this is a problem. And this is what we're calling it."

Over time there was a lot of pushback on gender nonconformity being an identity disorder. People were expressing that gender incongruence was not a mental disorder. In 2013 the diagnosis of gender identity disorder was replaced by gender dysphoria. So, they didn't remove it from the DSM completely, but they moved away from identity and instead focused on the level of distress that people with gender incongruence feel.

We see again and again that young kids whose gender identities are affirmed never experience the distress associated with gender dysphoria. They don't experience it.

The rest of the world uses the diagnosis codes in the ICD.† In ICD-11 what we call "gender dysphoria" is categorized as "sexual disorder," not a mental disorder, and the term used is "gender incongruence." This term, gender incongruence, aligns better with the transgender experience, because this is not a psychological problem. There is psychological impact to it. It's a medical problem that has psychological impact. So, the rest of the world uses the term gender incongruence.

So, in some senses it's an insurance thing. Historically, we

* *Diagnostic and Statistical Manual of Mental Disorders.*

† *International Classification of Diseases.*

didn't diagnose gender identity disorder or gender dysphoria unless someone needed access to medical care.

Cristina: While the terms are confusing, the experience of gender incongruence is a real thing. Can you describe that in your own words? What is the experience like?

Shawn: For those people who experience gender dysphoria, it's excruciating. There are two main aspects of it. We all have a mental map of what we expect to see in the mirror. And for those of us who were born trans, what we see in the mirror doesn't match our mental map. Many of us, though, when we are little kids, we tell our parents who we are. And if our parents affirm us, if they see us the way we see ourselves, we feel good. As little kids, this mirroring is a social experience. It often doesn't start becoming an actual problem with the mirror until adolescence, when your body starts changing. Or you start noticing yourself in the mirror and you're like, oh, I don't know if this is going to work. I have a distinct memory of standing and staring at the mirror and thinking something was wrong. I couldn't name it. I didn't know what it was. I would sometimes think, "Yeah, it'd be better if I were a guy," but I didn't know where to go with that. So, I actually didn't experience extreme distress. But for those who do, it's an existential panic.

So, for a little kid who tells their parents who they are, and their parents say, "Oh no honey, that's not who you are," and especially if they focus on the body parts, the kids start to focus on the parts as the thing that is messing with who they are. It sets up a dissonance with their body that I don't see in kids who are affirmed from a young age. Kids who are affirmed are mentally stable and they can rock with "I'm a girl with a penis." They're not too upset about it because they are seen for who they are, and the parts do not present a problem. But when adolescence comes and your body starts changing and you start not recognizing your own self in the mirror, that existential panic can set in again. And it's not just anxiety. It's full-on panic. Like, I don't exist. I can't even see myself, and you can't see me either. The sensation is that there is something really, really wrong here.

There's another piece to it, the second piece, which we call "gender noise." It goes beyond the dysphoria and has more to do with managing what you hear other people saying about you. These are the worries about walking in the world. Can I go in this bathroom? What are they going to do if I do? What if I tell someone I like them, but then they find out more about me and don't like that? There's this nonstop narrative that creates a lot of distress. This gender noise, it never goes away. It gets quieter and louder depending on the context. So, when you're more stressed it comes out more. You get a little more agitated and can get overwhelmed with negative self-talk.

Cristina: What you said about the mirror resonates so much for me. Jake has told me that when he was little and thought about learning to ride a bike he always saw a guy riding the bike. And he has said that when he imagined the future and growing up he saw a man riding the bike or a dad and his kids. He has talked to me about how he had to keep correcting himself. He said, "I would talk to myself and be like, no, no, no. That's not how this is going." And so, he just stopped thinking about the future.

Shawn: Yes, that's right. It's like we learn skills to manage the situation. For example, I learned never to look in a mirror. For a long time, I tried to do "girl" really, really well. If I was doing my hair or my make-up or getting dressed, I would look at just the part I was working on. Never the whole picture. Because when I looked at the whole picture, it was really upsetting.

But I want to go back to what you were saying about Jake and the future. Because it was that same thing, thinking about the future, that got me to transition. I was watching a movie called *You Don't Know Dick* and Jamison Green (a well-known trans male activist) was talking about his future. And he couldn't imagine himself as an old woman. He had no image for it. And I realized I didn't have an image for that either. I started thinking back and remembered an idea of myself as a park ranger with a moustache. Or a hermit on a mountain with a long beard. All these ideas of who I was going to end up as, and none of them were female. And in my dreams as a kid, I was a boy. An anatomically correct boy. When I was little I told my family I was a boy. I had arguments with them about it. They let me wear what I wanted to wear, which was an advantage. But my grandmother, for example, would always try to convince me about why I should want to be a girl. We would have these debates all the time.

Cristina: Wow. That is so interesting about your dreams. The image making is so deep.

Shawn: I think a lot of trans people shut down their future because they just can't imagine it. And this is a manifestation of gender incongruence. So, to get back to the diagnosis, this is what I look for. I look for the history of the person's incongruence.

Cristina: The history of incongruence sounds like the persistence aspect of the consistent, insistent, persistent quality that the gender dysphoria diagnosis describes. Can you talk a little bit how parents might be able to distinguish gender play from gender dysphoria?

Shawn: Well, in the diagnosis there is this length of time, six months. And that's okay, but usually I see a pattern of incongruence that is much longer, like a year or two. Now that isn't necessarily outwardly expressed. But we'll be talking, and things will show up that sound like feeling like they don't fit or feeling like they are very different. They are not sure why. There might be a little story about a teacher telling the boys to line up on one side of the room and the girls to line up on the other, and for the person there is confusion there. Like they don't know which side of the line to go to. Or feeling like they wanted to play in a certain area of the playground but knowing that they weren't really allowed to be doing that. A kid who is playing with gender is not so concerned about what they are allowed and not allowed to do. It's much less serious. But for someone who is really grappling with their identity, the details of who is allowed to do what, these are serious.

Cristina: Yes, I've heard Diane Ehrensaft say that kids with gender incongruence aren't playing with gender; they are working on gender.

Shawn: And what I see sometimes is that if there is gender stuff going on in the house and it's okay in the family there can be other contexts where it's more difficult. There can be kids who put other kids into a gender box. Or the kids can be cool, but there is a teacher who is not on board. Kids who are really questioning their identity at some level get that what's going on for them is serious. And there is a narrative out there, I think that everybody in school these days is nonbinary or trans, but we know that's not really true. When kids are dealing with issues of identity it is serious and they are vulnerable. If this weren't the case why would school climate surveys consistently show that gay and trans kids are bullied and harassed in the extreme, so much so that they are way more likely to drop out of school? Even in California.

Cristina: Given that it can be difficult for parents to distinguish between gender play and gender work, and also that the gender dysphoria diagnosis has so much nuance to it, what advice do you have for families when they are seeking the help of a gender therapist? What makes a good gender therapist? And what can families do if they can't find one where they live?

Shawn: So first off, this is why I started the TransFamily Alliance. I wanted to create an educational network and supportive community for parents, especially if they were in locations where there is not good access to gender-affirming care or if they could not afford a therapist. Because it costs a lot of money to go to therapy! But to go to your first question, you nailed something that's important to me, which is that for children, family needs to be included in the therapy process. There are not a lot of therapists out there who really include family and parents in the process. There are child psychologists who work with the parents collaterally. But ideally the therapist is working with the whole family.

A clinician should really be able to spend time with a parent and integrate the parent into what's happening. This is what I do in my practice, because look, the parent spends way more time with their kid than I do. It's much better for the child if the parent is involved in the process—so the ability to have someone who is willing to build rapport with you, not just with your kid. If they want to spend all their time with your kid and they just check in with you occasionally—they may be a great gender therapist, but they are not helping your whole system. I'm a family therapist, so it's my inclination to treat the whole system, and not all therapists are trained this way. But even if a gender therapist is not trained in family therapy they can work to have open communication with the parents and bring the parents along in the process. You want a therapist who is going to support your child and take a holistic family-centered perspective.

Letter 3

May 2019: The Incubator

When you came to me with the idea of building an incubator, I was skeptical. You wanted to give your sisters baby chicks for Easter this year, but I wasn't sure Alison would want them. For years raising chickens had been a local trend that she had rolled her eyes at. It irritated her to witness suburban families enacting this performance of hippy domesticity. Also, building your own incubator sounded overly ambitious to me, a complicated process better left to the professionals. But Easter was approaching, and I thought you were probably right to imagine that Alison wouldn't be able to resist a baby chick once she had it in her hands. Even for your 15-year-old sister who hated the idea of a family like ours pretending to have a farm, that yellow fuzzy baby animal would be lovable.

Before coming to me, you had put in a lot of planning. You'd calculated how to hatch the chicks to arrive by Easter, you'd scoped out the perfect place in our basement for the project, you'd scoured the internet for instructions, and you'd written down the list of what you'd need. A Styrofoam cooler, a light bulb attached to a dimmer, wire mesh, a thermometer and humidity detector, duct tape. I never told you this, but after you came to me, I checked online to see how much an already built incubator would cost, and for fifty bucks we could have had one at our doorstep the next day. But I appreciated your DIY attitude. So, we made a plan to go to the hardware store. A hundred and fifty dollars later we had a pile of supplies stacked in a corner in the basement.

With intense focus you cut and cobbled and duct-taped the incubator together. Soon enough, a white box, complete with ragged holes, a clip-on lamp, and a black wire tail, was operational. The rough-hewn object of a teenage boy's devotion. When I asked where you planned to get the eggs and you told me Trader Joe's (a local grocery store), I was incredulous. But you were adamant, and by then the plan seemed to be coming together, so who was I to get in your way? I told you we could go by the next day to pick some up. But you didn't want to wait.

Next thing I knew you were on your bike, your own twenty-dollar bill in your pocket, headed to Trader Joe's.

Over the course of the incubator project, I witnessed a potent desire in you, a yearning toward life and toward living. It felt familiar.

During the first visit we had at the pediatric gender clinic when you were 11, I experienced a flash of my own version of this desire. The doctor in the sweater was in the middle of telling you about the changes that taking testosterone would create. You were so excited. We had figured out how to get you the body that made sense to you, the broad shoulders, the flat chest, the deeper voice. You were stoked to learn that the added bonus of starting testosterone without ever having had a period was thought to be additional height. It turns out the growth plates in children's bones close faster during an estrogen puberty than during a testosterone puberty. This is part of the reason that men tend to grow taller than women. You were thrilled. The doctor's explanation made the body seem more pliable than I ever imagined.

To show him that I understood the biological concepts he was describing, I said, "So if someone who was born with a female body takes T before they complete their endogenous puberty, they could stop taking it and let their body proceed through the changes if they wanted to have a baby." I used that slang "T" instead of the actual word "testosterone" to signal my support and to emphasize that I got the whole gender affirmation concept. It was a kind of arrogance. I wanted him to perceive me as sophisticated, intelligent, and onboard.

But his face softened, and he shook his head "No."

"It's a permanent change," he said. "Children who go on blockers and then begin cross-sex puberty right away are permanently infertile." His voice stayed steady, like a chord in C major—calm, strong, but not unkind. My stomach dropped. How had I not understood this beforehand? With the facts laid out before me it made sense, but none of the psychologists or other clinicians who had talked to me about gender dysphoria had ever mentioned this. After the shock of it, I felt so stupid for not figuring it out myself. The doctor read the distress on my face and handed me a box of tissues.

I pulled one out and pressed it on my face. You said, "Mom, don't cry."

In my mind's eye I imagined your ovaries shriveling, their pink insides wrinkling up like dried figs. A phrase from a Sharon Olds poem about her daughter flew through me—her purse full of eggs—would there be no purse of eggs for you?

A memory so old it felt ancient rose up in my awareness. I

was eight months pregnant with you and had drawn a hot bath. I lowered my heavy body into the warm water and allowed my arms to hang over the side of the tub while I squatted. The weight of my belly shifted from my low back into the bowl of my hips. The fullness of your baby body pressed between my thighs, your head stretched and pulled at the folds of my most tender skin. I felt a heel nudge me from the inside. I knew then I was a world, an entire galaxy even. I was an entire life wrapped around another entire life. It was a powerful pleasure that consumed me.

Before becoming pregnant, I understood I had a desire for children, but there was another drive inside me that I did not know I had. I don't think I knew it existed until I experienced it myself. In the process of trying to become pregnant, I felt an urge coming to a crescendo. Maybe it was how mountain climbers felt when they heeded the call of their next 14,000-foot peak. The obsession, the staking out and planning, the attraction of the challenge itself—of accomplishing a difficult, although rationally baseless, corporeal feat—simply for the thrill of it. I had never heard of the desire for pregnancy spoken about this way, as something a woman might just want to experience for herself—for the pleasure and for the swagger earned when a body attained its own heroic victories.

I knew not everyone had the urge to become pregnant, but did I want you to have this pleasure? Was I mourning that you might not have it? Of course. I wanted you to have every good thing I could conjure. Even then I understood I was projecting my own longings onto you, but underneath the projection I knew I had tapped into an embodied experience that was important to the conversation with the doctor and to your decision to start testosterone. Whereas I felt confident you knew your gender and had known it for a long time, I did not feel as confident that you understood your own desires about reproduction.

And there was something distressing to me about the doctor's quiet calm. He didn't say anything about research that was on the horizon. He didn't express any condolences for your loss. He seemed relatively unperturbed by a side effect of gender affirmation that I perceived as grave. In my upset I read his neutrality as lack of concern, and his disregard shook my trust in the clinical protocol we were about to follow. How could I have been expected to wholeheartedly embrace a process that required robbing you of your reproductive choice, a right that generations of women had fought to prove was a fundamental human right? Was I just supposed to accept that this was "the way things were done?"

At the time of our first appointment at the gender clinic, the most long-standing clinics in the country had been seeing patients for less than ten years, which meant that the very first patients who went straight from blockers to their cross-sex hormones were only just beginning their twenties. I trusted the experience that was transpiring in your life. It was tangible and very real to me. But I had not yet decided how I felt about the authorities we were consulting. How confident could they be that dismissing the fertility of a generation of trans people was not going to have a negative impact? And who in the medical community was pushing for a more complete, holistic solution? At the end of the appointment, when they showed me the various release forms I would have to sign if you took testosterone, I felt isolated and angry. Each form made it very clear that Dad and I were legally accountable for all of this, and yet I knew that we were about to participate in a process, that by most standards, especially when it comes to minors, was still cutting-edge.

After that first appointment at the gender clinic, I started to ask questions about the possibility of preserving your reproductive choices somehow. If your hormone blockers were stopped, and you experienced your estrogen puberty, eggs could be retrieved the same way adult women retrieve their eggs for IVF treatments. But I know it is untenable for you to stop your blockers and let your body take on a female shape. As much as I want you to avoid choosing between your identity and your fertility, I cannot imagine asking you to go through physical changes that would be so hard on you.

Your endocrinologist mentioned the possibility of ovarian extraction, suggesting in one of your regular appointments that we could consider surgically removing an ovary, and then freezing it until you were ready to think about becoming a parent. Fifteen years into the future she thought maybe the technology to grow an egg from that tissue might be available. But thinking about cutting out an ovary made my stomach feel the way it did in the occasional moments when I accidentally imagined you or your sisters injured and bleeding from a car wreck. The blood, the wounded skin, the yolky softness of your internal organs. The recoil away from the idea was primal. Still, I was glad she mentioned it, because it was at least heartening that your options were on her mind, even if they did seem far-fetched and extreme.

Over the years I'd wondered why the fertility of trans kids had not been a priority in the gender affirmation process. Clearly part of the reason was scientific. While the ability to retrieve and freeze oocytes from adult women is well understood, no one we'd met had discussed fertility preservation options for young people who have not yet experienced puberty. This reality, combined with the huge numbers of trans youth who attempt suicide because of the distress caused by gender dysphoria, made a strong case for de-prioritizing this secondary effect of early gender transitions. It is certainly better to save the life of a trans person than to save their ability to produce their own biological children. But the trade-off keeps me up at night.

Given that your mental health has been so steady, I hate that Dad and I are in the position of having to make this choice for your adult self. We'll do it if we must, but it's not something I am inclined to accept easily. I can't shake the sense that trans people's reproductive rights and reproductive desires are not well understood and are likely under-protected. While gender affirmation is the right treatment for gender dysphoria, it does not necessarily follow that the process is as robust and compassionate as it needs to be.

Living in Silicon Valley has taught me that successful technology comes to life in the imaginations of innovators. And of the clinicians we've met over the years—the gender therapists, the adolescent pediatricians, the pediatric endocrinologists—no one strikes me as having the necessary creative spark that would drive them to see your reproductive future. The clinicians we work with are in the business of saving young trans people's lives. The work is urgent, and in a way, crisis driven. I haven't yet encountered the hunger and curiosity, the squinted eyes trying to make out the shape of the future as it emerges from the horizon that I've seen in the eyes of the entrepreneurs and innovators Dad and I know. Consequently, I worry that your own ideas about your future are sometimes more constrained than necessary. I know that if someone were to give you the choice between having your own babies or growing up as a man, there would be no doubt about what you would choose. The question is, do you really have to make that choice, or are there other options we have not yet heard about or that are just about to arrive?

Your incubator project has reignited my sense that I need to think harder about your fertility options. Witnessing your yearning for baby chicks, I've wondered if I've been witnessing a teenage boy's version of reproductive desire, of that same deep urge I had not even known I had until I experienced it. But I really don't know. I don't know who could talk to me about reproductive desire in the trans community. I don't have much of an idea about what reproductive rights mean in concrete terms for you as a teenager or as an adult. I know people become parents at all ages and stages and in all kinds of different ways. And I don't mean to over emphasize the biological version of family building. But I do want to take a stand for your agency, for the idea that choosing the way you become a parent, if you want to become a parent someday, is a choice that belongs to your adult self, not Dad and me.

When you came into my bedroom because you thought you needed to get new eggs for the incubator, I asked if you had candled them to see how they were doing. (Did this tip you off to the fact that I had started to do my own research about growing chicks?) You had, and you told me they looked like they weren't growing. I reminded you it had only been a little while and I wasn't sure it was time for us to give up on them yet. I suggested that we wait until after spring break to replace them. Your face and shoulders slumped. We would not have chicks for Easter. You were disappointed, but I told you there are some things in life you just can't rush. You heaved a big sigh. Time refused to obey your wishes. Puberty was approaching too fast; the eggs were growing too slowly. So little was on your terms.

Waiting until after spring break meant I was in charge of caring for the eggs while you went on your school camping trip. Before you left, you took me down to the basement and squatted down next to your incubator. You pointed to small circles you had drawn on each egg and showed me how they helped track how far the egg had rotated through its revolution. You reminded me to be gentle, and then looked up to emphasize, "but also quick," so that the heat would not escape. The first night I turned them myself, I lifted the flat lid of the Styrofoam box where the five white eggs each hung in their own mesh hammocks. Hot air swirled around them, and the warming lamp threw off a hopeful golden light. I turned each egg a quarter of the way around. Then I closed the lid to preserve the warm air, just like you told me to. On my way up the stairs, I looked over my shoulder at your incubator. The glowing white box lit up the dark like a teenage boy's ode to the moon.

When you came back from your camping trip, we continued turning the eggs for a few more days, but still nothing happened inside your incubator. We discussed where we might order new eggs from the internet, but by then we were caught up in the rush of the school calendar, bobbing along in the rush of events that would deliver us to the end of the school year.

REFLECTION QUESTIONS

- When you consider the medical aspect of transition for trans people, what questions do you have? Do you experience anxiety thinking about a medical transition for your child? If so, what aspects of medical transition concern you most?

- What outside sources—TV shows, articles, recently enacted local laws—echo your concerns? What level of trust do you have in these sources? How do these sources impact your day-to-day life?
- What sources do you trust to share accurate information with you? Consider doctors, psychologists, fellow parents of trans children, trans adults you know, educators, or counselors. Who will you reach out to for help in finding accurate information? If you do not have a source you feel like you can trust, where might you turn for support?
- How concerned are you about your child's reproductive future? What organization or person might be able to connect you with cutting-edge information about reproductive choices and family building in the trans community?

Letter 4

May 2019: Fresh Starts

After spring break, I received a call from your advisor at school. We were coming to the end of your first school year living as a boy named Jake. A few teachers knew your gender history, but as far as anyone else knew, you were just another boy in the class. This was the first time that your gender history was ever invisible to the people around you. We knew that in our small community you would never be able to go totally "stealth," that is, you would never be able to keep your gender history entirely out of view for the long term. But one of the reasons you had changed schools was to see what it felt like for you to live completely as a boy.

Tom, your advisor, called me that afternoon because one of your ally-teachers had broken up a lunchtime debate you were having with a classmate. The two of you were arguing about the use of people's affirmed pronouns. Your classmate was adamant that facts did not care about people's feelings and that people didn't just "get" to say they were female or male because they "felt like it." You tried to explain to him what pronouns meant to trans people, but he wouldn't budge. As he repeated, "Facts don't care about people's feelings," you repeated, "What did a trans person ever do to you?" which is when the teacher broke things up. According to your advisor, most of the other seventh graders who had been sitting at your lunch table had abandoned the debate to avoid the conflict. After he and I talked we decided to reach out to the head of school at your new school, to discuss a strategy for de-escalating the conflict, which sounded like it was not going to let up.

The phrase, "Facts don't care about feelings," had a catchy ring to it, so after hanging up with Tom I looked it up online. It was a quote from a conservative pundit named Ben Shapiro. My search returned a slew of videos in which Shapiro voiced an impassioned defense of straight white men, a group he perceived as being under cultural attack. Shapiro was well spoken (he had graduated from Harvard Law School) and handsome. It depressed me to discover that his books regularly appeared on *The New York Times* bestseller list. How I wished people were reading about trans lives in books by trans authors—books like *Amateur*, by Thomas Page McBee or *Pass with Care* by Cooper Lee Bombardier, or *Psychopomps* by Alex DiFrancesco. These well-written, compelling books offered persuasive first-person perspectives that challenged Shapiro's incendiary, sound-bite-driven punditry.

Before Dad and I had officially enrolled you at your new school, I warned the head of school, Sam, that something like this would inevitably crop up. At your previous school, we had learned the hard way that even in the Bay Area, where so many people took pride in their progressive politics, transphobia existed just under the surface. People in our local community seemed to fall into roughly three categories. Most were supportive. They wanted trans people to have rights, but they had little or no practice stepping into a conflict to support someone who might be vulnerable. These were good people who froze when they experienced interpersonal tension. Another group of people said they were supportive, but weren't. They said they had no problem with trans people, but they didn't want their own son having a sleepover with you. And they didn't want you in the boys' bathroom or locker room. My interactions with people we knew in this group had been especially maddening because they thought they supported you. Their attitude was "You do you, but not in my space." They didn't get that restricting your access to public spaces like restrooms counted as discrimination.

Thankfully there were a small handful of people who truly understood what was at stake for you. They supported you, and they had practice intervening on behalf of others who were culturally or politically vulnerable. When I first met Sam, I had a feeling he would be in this last category. He was passionate about the school's inclusivity statement and told me that if a family was not able to support it or did not want to support it, there were a lot of other schools for them to choose from. He said, "A family that chooses us, chooses inclusivity, full stop." That phrase "full stop" signaled to me that he would not be intimidated by potential conflict. His approach had contributed to our family's decision to move you into a new community.

It had not been an easy decision. You had attended your previous school since you were in kindergarten. Both of your sisters attended the same school, and we had a wide network of families with whom we were close. You played flag football on a team coached by one of your friend's dads. Your LEGO® robotics team was led by a mom who had a boy in your grade. And I had my own set of friendships that had grown through my volunteer work. You and your sisters had grown up in that community, and, even as your gender evolved over the years, I never imagined leaving.

Of all our friends and connections, Josh was the star. He was your best friend. You laughed at the same jokes. You built ships out of LEGO. You played Star Wars and a game you called "Dog family." You both liked martial arts. You moved similarly, like wind-up bumper cars, pulling away from one another then ramming into each other, or into the wall or onto the primary-colored rug on the floor of your first-grade classroom. Your relationship with him was the heartbeat of your waking hours—what you played together at recess, which of your afternoon activities included him, what our weekend plans were with his family—these were the rhythms that organized your days. So, when you got your first boyish haircut, showing it to Josh was the single most important thing on your mind.

When we arrived on campus that first day of first grade you tore your hand from mine and ran ahead to find him. My hand tingled with emptiness where yours had been while I tried to catch up with you. Through the doorway of your classroom, I caught a glimpse of you buzzing past a few clusters of kids toward the back of the room where he stood. As I saw you heading toward Josh, I decided to step inside and watch what was about to happen. You zoomed right up to him, screaming his name, and jutting your chin forward. I remember how he looked back at you with a wrinkled forehead and squinted eyes. I can still hear how you squealed, "Josh, it's me!"

At the sound of your voice, my insides turned weak and fragile like eggshells. Your hair had been short for a couple of weeks by then, and it already seemed so much a part of you that I had forgotten its newness. We still called you by the name we gave you when you were born. We still used female pronouns. In our immediate family, you were the same person you had always been—just with short hair. But in the instant that Josh did not recognize you, I understood the change was more profound than I realized. I did not know what it meant to you exactly, but I could see in your face how important it was. So much depended on Josh right then, so much more than was reasonable to expect from one first grade boy. You locked eyes with him and puffed out your chest, offering your whole self. A blush rose in his cheeks, and he took a step back. I had taken it as a given that Josh would accept you in a boy's haircut, but I saw then how badly I had misjudged what it could mean between you.

I held my breath. My pulse pounded in my ears. I silently repeated one desperate word. Please—please please please please please.

Then his mouth spread into a huge smile. His shoulders lifted up toward his ears. Suddenly you were both shrieking, two wiggly first graders crumbling into peals of laughter, rolling around on the blue carpet. You both got up, and you looked at Josh with your palm pulled back for a high five. When he pushed his palm towards yours and they clapped together, you said something remarkable, "Dude, we're the same now." Then off you went, a pair of matching boys.

That day was the first time I started to get an inkling of what was at stake for you, although it would be years before I understood the full scope of it. Right then I understood that you wanted to look like a boy. On occasion I asked you if you wanted to be a boy, and you often responded by saying that you liked looking like a boy on the outside, but that you wanted to keep being a girl inside your heart. For the rest of the school year, it pleased you when people mistook you and Josh for twins.

Once your hair was short, people who did not know you

personally always mistook you for a boy. At first Dad and I corrected them, but it quickly became easier to just let it go. When a server or a clerk at a store called you bud, or buddy, or sir, or little man, you always sat up a little bit taller. We asked you how you felt about it, and you said you kind of liked it. But if I ever asked if you wanted to be a boy, which I did after psychologists suggested you might have gender dysphoria, you told me you didn't.

As time passed, I wondered if Dad and I had made you wear dresses or behave more like your sisters, whether you would have said you wanted to be a boy. We gave you a lot of latitude that other families might not have. We let you choose boys' clothes. We let you cut your hair short. When I tried to sign you up for softball and you insisted on baseball, we got you signed up for baseball. We even let you swim bare-chested in boys' swim trunks. The boys' bathing suit was the biggest stretch for us. But when we saw the way you cowered in a girls' swimsuit compared to the way you blasted into the ocean in your swim trunks, the decision had not been that difficult. If you had been a boy who wanted to dress and act like a girl, I'm ashamed to admit, it probably would have felt harder. It is still so much more difficult for people who are assigned male at birth (kids or adults) to negotiate the line between femininity and masculinity. And I'm certain, families in our community would have put up more barriers, but as it was, they were happy to go along with the idea of a boy-ish girl.

As it often happens between mothers, I had become good friends with several of your friends' moms. We loved to talk about movies and politics and books. Ours was the kind of friendship that allowed for delicious gossip and honest reveals about the way we were flailing as parents or as people.

You were able to be yourself with your friends from elementary school. You had sleepovers at their houses. You wore your swim trunks in their families' hot tubs. You played soccer and baseball and flag football on the same teams. Our families ate out at favorite restaurants on weekends and went on a beach vacation together. For years, the fact that you had a female body and used a girl's name didn't seem to matter. But in middle school, things changed.

I've gone back and forth a thousand times about whether or not to relay these stories to you. For one, it is really hard to explain what happened without making it sound like I was part of a cabal of gossiping adults who were more like middle schoolers than the actual middle schoolers. And second, I don't like the thought of disrupting the happy memories you still have about this time. But what feels important is for you to know the truth, as best as I can tell it. And the truth is that it did sometimes feel like being back in middle school again, but worse because of the impact these interactions had on you. These experiences shattered my understanding of the community we were a part of back then. On the whole our family has taken a very positive view of the world and your place in it. But for you to be safe, it's important for us to grapple with the complicated reality, instead of hiding in the bubble of false acceptance I let myself believe in for so long.

An incident that signaled how things were changing happened at the end of fifth grade—at a springtime playdate with water guns. Do you remember it? It was so hot that day. You were with some of your friends at Sean's house. Sean's mom, Darla, texted me from the playdate and told me that all of you were outside soaking each other. She wanted to know how I felt about you playing shirtless with the boys. I was surprised because we had gone swimming with them so many times. Darla knew I let you take off your shirt. But since you and the boys were all getting bigger, maybe she was starting to feel uncomfortable. At the time, the only thing that registered was a feeling of surprise. She knew I let you go shirtless, so why was she texting me? I replied that it was fine with me. Then she texted "Okay." I picked you up later that afternoon and didn't think about the playdate again for a long time.

The summer came and went, and except for running into her once while I was on a walk, I didn't see her again until your first day of sixth grade. After I took your picture in front of the school sign like we did every year, and you had run off with a gang of your friends, I approached a huddle of moms in the school yard. Darla was off to the left of the group. A few of my other friends approached me with hugs and asked how our summer had been. But Darla hardly made eye contact. She didn't even say hello. Had something happened between us that I had not realized? I flipped through my memories of our last few interactions. The only thing that came to me was the playdate, but I couldn't quite believe she would stop talking to me without a discussion first. If I had somehow hurt her feelings or done something she didn't like, I assumed she would have at least said something.

But the scene at school drop-off chilled me in a way I couldn't quite understand, and I didn't linger. Walking away from the school yard, I brought my hands to my face and let out a few sobs. How I felt and what I thought did not match up. I chastised myself and pulled myself back together. I needed to stop overreacting; it was probably nothing. I sent her a text to ask if everything was okay. Her reply was curt. She told me she needed "distance." As I stood next to my car reading the text my stomach lurched. For months I had been looking forward to that moment when Darla and I could squeeze in a coffee date for ourselves. The fall looked suddenly bleak to me, and I hoped that your first day back was going better than mine.

I hoped things would shift in the weeks ahead, but they didn't. Around this time, your connections with friends outside of school started to dry up. By wintertime of sixth grade, you were isolated and lonely. I felt crazed by my inability to pull together playdates. It took me months to figure out which moms I could call, and which moms would not return my calls. Over Halloween, a gathering of your friends was organized, but you were not included. I scrambled and called your friend Max's mom, Emma, to see if you could go over with Max. She said yes, but when we got there it felt awkward, like we were dropping in on the party uninvited (which of course we were). At the end of the term, Max invited you to a Christmas party at his house on the last day of school before winter break. You called me from the school office to ask if you could go home with him. I hadn't received an invite from Emma and things with some of the moms had been feeling so uncomfortable. I told you I needed to check in with his mom to make sure it was okay.

When I called to find out whether you were really invited to her house, she said you were not. She told me her house was not big enough to hold a big group. You called me again from school to find out if you could go to the party and I had to tell you that you couldn't. Relaying this message to you was one of the hardest things I've ever had to do as a mom. When I picked you up from school you asked me, "Do they really not have room for one more kid?" I pulled you to my chest and wrapped my arms tight around you as you wept.

I remember another time when one of my mom friends from school, Mary, invited me to have lunch with her out of the blue.

As we ate our food, I heard Mary say, "You know about the outdoor ed, right? The tent thing?"

I had not heard anything about the "tent thing."

Your small school was known for its outdoor education program, and for years you had been tenting with the boys on these trips. The teachers and parents in the community all knew that your best friends were boys, and because you were having trouble sleeping even when you were at home, the school had agreed to support you by allowing you to sleep with your friends on these overnight trips. In preparation for any of these trips, students were given the opportunity to name a few friends they would be happy tenting with. The staff made sure that every student was with at least one of their choices. In your case, the other families whose kids would tent with you were called to make sure they were okay with their son sharing sleeping arrangements. Since you took a few camping trips a year, I felt confident any kinks in the process had been ironed out in your younger grades, and that the system worked well for everyone involved.

But on the most recent trip, the school had placed you in a tent with another boy, apparently without ever reaching out to his parents. I would not have anticipated this being a problem because we knew the family well and you had previously had sleepovers with their son. But for Mary it was a problem. A big problem. Discussing the event, about which I had known nothing, our conversation escalated until she finally blurted out that she was grateful it wasn't her son, Jackson who had shared the tent with you and that she would never let Jackson share a tent with you on a school trip.

Her admission hit me like a punch. I couldn't understand what she was saying to me. You and Jackson had been friends for years. I felt like I was talking to someone I didn't even know. My thinking went gauzy. Across the table, Mary looked slanted and gray and very far away from me. I felt dizzy, and my hands and armpits went clammy with cold sweat.

Her voice got louder then and she asked me if I had ever thought of what would happen if you took your shirt off in a tent and a boy touched you. "Well of course you wouldn't know what it feels like. Because you're not actually raising a son. You have no idea how dangerous it is to be a boy right now." Then she started to lecture me about raising boys and how vulnerable they were to being blamed for anything. With puberty on the horizon, sleepovers felt much riskier. I thought back to the various incidents over the past year and wondered how many of them had been motivated by similar concerns. Mary thought this was all common sense. I wondered if other parents shared Mary's anxiety, even if they would never come right out and say it because they were worried that this perspective would not be well received in our progressive community. Mary, however, had no problem saying the quiet part out loud.

I had mistakenly assumed Mary understood more about gender than she did. In my mind she, like most parents around us, assumed you were on a different gender path. I asked her point blank, "Isn't it obvious that she is more or less a boy?" Looking back, I can write that phrase and understand how ridiculous it would have sounded to someone like Mary, who didn't have much reason to think about gender diversity or gender dysphoria. I am sure she thought I was a lunatic. But our family was so ensconced in our own way of thinking and interacting with you that the sentence, "She is a boy," no longer had any cognitive dissonance. This was my big mistake—I had completely lost track of how out of step we had become. I had no idea that things that seemed normal to us seemed like huge impositions to other people.

Her reply to this was, "Think about it," she said, "the kids are at a curious age. You let your daughter walk around bare chested. What would happen to my son if, out of curiosity, he accidentally touched her nipple?" The way she talked about touching made my stomach go weak. The word nipple echoed inside me. There are so many other ways she could have put it, but nipple, it was so prurient. The sound of it repeated over and over so that the inside of my head felt like a clanging bell.

Up until this conversation I had not let myself believe that the social trouble we were having had anything to do with your gender. In retrospect, it felt like a kind of negligence that I had failed to read how your gender was impacting other families, but we had gotten along well for so many years, I assumed our personal relationships trumped any preconceived ideas people had about gender.

I sat stunned as Mary told me how much she supported you. "But" she explained, "if your family is going to do the whole gender switch thing," we would need to educate the parents in the community. She gave me the sense that there had been conversations about us, and that the community, or at least a group in the community, agreed that our family could not just spring a new gender identity on them without involving them in the process. Whether or not there was a larger conversation going on at school, I could not know, but it was not hard to imagine Mary commiserating with other parents about the situation they imagined I had forced on their sons.

To be told that she supported you and that she thought of you as a girl wounded me, and it would have devastated you if you had heard her say it. She could not imagine that the two ideas—that she supported you and that she thought of you as a girl—were mutually exclusive. Then again, it was becoming clear to me that she needed education I just assumed she had. The pressure she was exerting on me to take responsibility for her learning added to my hurt and felt unreasonable. I debated her about this for a little bit before making my excuses and leaving.

I drove home in a world that felt new and unfamiliar. I got lost on roads I have been driving for 20 years. Stop lights looked blurry and blinked unpredictably. When I finally pulled up in front of our old house, it no longer felt like ours. Its faded bricks and paned windows arranged in perfect symmetry. The front lawn with its low hedge that made two postage stamp gardens. The peaked roof that seemed to imply two opposing lines could find their harmonious resolution. All that tradition and idealism had made sense to a version of me that no longer existed. The house no longer fit. Our friends no longer felt like friends. And worst of all, the most unfixable piece of it was that the school, by forgetting to tell a family that you were going to share a tent with their child, had lost the trust of the people who we most needed to trust in the school's judgment. I knew then that it was time to change. We needed to start over in a new school, and probably also a new neighborhood, where we would be known from the start as a family with two daughters and a son.

A few weeks later when we sang "The Circle Game" at your sister's eighth grade graduation, I looked across the auditorium, first to her and then to you, where you sat with your class. You and I were both crying big heaving sobs while we tried to sing. "We can't return, we can only look behind from where we came and go round and round and round in the circle game."

It's hard to think about this experience all over again. But, like painful experiences often do, it taught me a lot and prepared me for the conflict that cropped up at your new school. Even in the progressive area where we live, it was naive to expect that everyone we knew and met would be onboard with the way we handled your gender. Parents who knew your history needed more education than they had, and I had underestimated how this need increased as parents' anxiety about sexuality became more pronounced in middle school. I also realized that in our previous school community, where accommodations had been made specifically for you, we had made a mistake. Even though the school had a diversity statement, the special arrangements that had been set up for you were not rooted in that policy. Instead, they relied on the assumption that parents in the community were generally progressive and inclined to be nice to each other's children. With your gender history out in the open, you needed more rigorous, mission-based support. I never imagined we would need it when we were surrounded by people who I thought of as friends. But once I did, I felt as if I had spent your early years fabricating a gender fantasy that left you more vulnerable than I should have ever allowed you to be. We changed schools in part to address this mistake that I had made.

After your advisor, Tom, called me about your recess debate, it was impossible not to rehash how things had fallen apart in our previous school community. I hung up the phone and sighed. My shoulders slumped and a blanket of fatigue weighed me down. I was not surprised by what was happening. And even though I had accepted the reality of pockets of intolerance, it was exhausting to anticipate the way things could fall apart. We'd worked so hard to get you into a better situation. And although I had never allowed myself to believe that moving and changing schools would be a fool-proof plan, I still wished for a longer stretch of time without conflict.

When these issues arose, Tom and Sam both had your back. Sam made it clear that you being cornered into these sorts of debates was unacceptable to him personally and at odds with the school's mission. I think they expected me to be angry. But I wasn't. For once I was not caught by surprise. I asked them if they had checked in with you, and Tom said he had, and that you were getting a little tired out from the debates. I asked specifically if Tom could tell whether you were afraid. He had asked you about this and told me you felt safe, but you were also ready for the conversations to simmer down. When I talked with you later, you confirmed this.

But after our last experience, I knew that framing these kinds of conflicts as a problem between you and another student was a set-up for more conflict. It was important to frame them as being at odds with the school's inclusion policy. I was keen for the community we'd worked so hard to build at your new school to have the best chance of remaining intact.

I asked Sam whether he had ever had any school meetings or parent meetings about the school's diversity statement, specifically how it impacted the community's relationship to free speech. He hadn't. The whole community deserved more information about what it meant to support this policy. This made sense to him. He was clear that the "facts don't care about your feelings" attitude made a community less inclusive because it made life less safe for trans people. He also told me he planned to talk to the teachers, students, and parents about the inclusion statement.

Tom suggested that all the teachers in school could post a printed version of the inclusivity statement in every classroom.

Over a few days, the school environment transformed. Not only were the inclusivity statements posted in every classroom, but each teacher also led a conversation about what the statement meant in their specific class. Parents received a powerful letter about inclusion, which included the phrase, "Free speech is not free of consequences." I never anticipated that a school could move so quickly and decisively on a complex topic. On the outside, I felt cautiously optimistic; on the inside I felt like a wrung-out dishrag. Would you always have to deal with so much social stress?

REFLECTION QUESTIONS

- A person who is questioning their gender or living into their affirmed gender for the first time needs a supportive community. Who makes up this supportive community for your child? How diverse in age and gender is this group of people? If, for example, your child does not have gender-diverse peers, where might you go to connect with a group of peers?
- Think of the different environments where your child spends extended amounts of time. How supported is your child's gender identity in each of these contexts? If there is an environment that you perceive as not supportive, what would need to change? Who do you know who might be able to help you make a plan? Is there a clinician

who can make a call to an educator? Do you have a good friend who is an ally who can talk to a troop leader? Is there a fellow parent who has been through a similar experience who can help you make a plan?

- Parents of trans children and teens often have no choice but to become ambassadors for the gender-diverse community, and as such we encounter people who are in different places on their journey to understand gender and on their journey to stand up for injustice. This work can be rewarding, and it also can be exhausting. How do you conserve your energy in this work? How do you differentiate between people who are open to your family's story and people whose minds will never be changed? What resources and strategies have led to "light bulb" moments for people in your community?
- The previous chapter talked about different circumstances in which our family navigated conflict successfully and unsuccessfully. Success for us was linked to de-personalizing the conflict my son was experiencing, and calling on our community to act on core values they had already agreed were important. What core values at your local club, school, or neighborhood can be activated to improve your child's wellbeing? If you belong to a religious community, what core values of your belief system can be activated to support your child, and who are the individuals who can influence the community on your child's behalf?

Interview

Alex DiFrancesco on Trans Mental Wellbeing

Alex DiFrancesco is a multi-genre writer and transmasc person (they/them). They are the author of *Transmutation*, *All City*, and *Psychopomps*. Their work has appeared in *The New York Times*, *The Washington Post*, *Tin House*, Pacific Standard, Eater, Brevity, and more. They are the recipient of grants and fellowships from PEN America, Sundress Academy for the Arts, and other organizations.

Cristina: Alex, talk to me about your personal story and your mental health journey. How do you think your story could support other people?

Alex: I grew up in not only a deeply transphobic family, but also a family where there was physical violence. So, it was a dual thing for me when I was growing up to be gaslit, both about my gender identity and the violence in the house. My mom's storyline was that this kind of thing never even happened. That sort of gaslighting from the jump rocks you.

It was exacerbated by the fact that I was very expressive about being transgender from when I was a young age. I didn't have the word transgender, but I was very vocal about the fact that I did not feel like a girl and that I was way more comfortable wearing boys' clothes, and with the idea of boys' haircuts. Up to a certain point that was tolerated as cute kid eccentric stuff. And then it hit a point where my family was clear that, no, this is wrong, and you can't do this, you cannot behave this way. You are not allowed to cut your hair, and you are not allowed to wear boys' clothes. I mention both things, because they are pretty classic examples of gaslighting and they're both examples of abuse. And a lot of people don't think that denying trans kids their gender experience is abuse, but it absolutely is. Because it creates the same sort of problems that other kinds of gaslighting does, as extended studies on the effects of gaslighting have been proven to show. Over the last couple of decades, complex post-traumatic stress disorder (PTSD) has been used frequently to describe this kind of extended abuse. It destabilizes your sense of self, which can create long-term depression. And it can also create an inability to test reality, because you have been told so firmly and for so long that your experience is just not right. So, you lose the ability to trust what you know and believe is right.

I have struggled with mental illness since I was a teenager. I've been diagnosed with chronic depression, complex PTSD, bipolar disorder, anxiety, generalized anxiety. I think at one point they even tried to put a schizoaffective label on me too. My mental health was just so bad that I kept getting these diagnoses all over the place. Nobody could quite figure out what was going on. And then, when I was 30, I came out of the closet as a trans person. And it's kind of amazing how much realizing this part of myself that I had kept tucked away and hidden opened the doors for better mental health, and for me, for being able to trust myself again.

I mention all this to say that not affirming a trans person's identity is a form of abuse that can carry through somebody's whole life.

Cristina: Would you say that the way transphobia invalidates a person's internal reality destabilizes a person's mental health?

Alex: I'd say it's a good part of it. And it's a good part of what happens to people who experience transphobia in their home environment. Also, not everyone will go into the closet, but then that can cause other issues. For example, the rate of homelessness in this population is much higher than for cisgender people. Seventeen per cent of sexual minorities experience homelessness in their lifetimes, which is more than twice the general population. So, you don't go in the closet, but now you're out on the street. Out there on a snowy night, looking for any old creep who comes along to take you home with them, because you need a place to sleep. And I've seen that sort of thing firsthand. I used to volunteer with the Ali Forney Center in New York, and the stories that kids will tell there are just tragic and seeing kids walking in with broken arms and other injuries. That's a whole other piece of mental health.

Cristina: What would you want parents of trans kids to know, in terms of supporting their children's mental health? What kinds of things are helpful, and what kinds of things are harmful?

Alex: I had a little neighbor who lived across the hall from me for the last year, and one day, my tiny neighbor asked her mom, "How do you know if you're they/them?" Her mom told her that you just feel it inside you, because you know who you are inside. And my little neighbor said, "Okay," and then she was they/them, and three days later, she was back to she/her. She changed her name to Mr. Rainbow in those three days. Parents get so hung up on the idea that maybe it's just a phase. So what if it is? It's alright if your kid decides for three days to be Mr. Rainbow, who uses they/them pronouns. How is it any different from your kid deciding they want to be an artist or a boxer or a sports star? Kids go through phases, and then they grow out of some things. For other kids who are trans, that is a big part of their identity, and they will be consistent about it. And I think parents will know the difference between a fleeting sort of phase and the idea that this part of the child's identity will hold on. What I would say is to let your kid be the guide. A lot of parents question the reality of children, but kids test reality all the time. That's a thing that happens. And is it the worst thing if your kid wants to take a moment or a period of time to test out a different gender? Why would that be a bad thing? We need to get more used to the idea that there's more than two genders, and that there are many approaches to gender.

Letter 5

June 2019: Back to My Roots

The spring has been exhausting. And so no, I did not want to go to my 25th Harvard reunion. But one of my classmates called and convinced me I should. She tried to sell me on who was going to be there and what a fun party the 25th was. Neither of these points was a big draw for me. But hearing the voice of my old friend on the phone felt like turning the lights on in the attic. So much of what I had studied in college was packed up inside me. And when I heard my friend's voice, I felt how much what I learned then has been shaping the way I think about your gender. Twenty-five years ago, all the feminist theory I studied for my degree was theoretical, but now all that theory has more real-life impact than I ever thought it would.

Cambridge, Massachusetts is never prettier than in late spring when the lilacs are in bloom. And as soon as I arrived on campus and caught their scent, my mood about returning changed. I wished I had brought you with me. I wanted to walk you through the gates of Radcliffe, into its small, gated courtyard. I wanted you to feel the protection of those hundreds-of-years-old brick buildings. I wanted to usher you through the doors of the Schlesinger Library, which houses the largest collection of primary sources about American gender history in the US, and show you how I used to stash my backpack in a locker in the front hall before I signed into the archival room. I wanted to show you an archival crate full of dusty papers—maybe the old mimeographs printed by NOW in the sixties, or handwritten notes from Gloria Steinem, Betty Friedan, or Barbara Seaman, all documents I had studied. I wished you could stand next to me on the front steps of the library and feel the steady hold of tradition and admire the charm of a bright green lawn in the middle of a bustling city, adorning it like a gem.

I had not stepped foot onto the Radcliffe campus since I was a college student. The amount of time that had passed was almost twice your own lifetime. The small collection of buildings a few blocks outside the more imposing Harvard yard was once my safest refuge. Returning, I experienced the passage of time like an illusion, a snap of an old magician's fingers then a doubling. I was struck by the simultaneous sense that I had been on campus just yesterday and that many years had passed, as if a huge amount of time had accumulated overnight. The college-aged me next to my middle-aged self. The younger woman took in my familiar yet foreign form, my wider waist, my creased hands with fingers that curved slightly like her grandmother's had, my skin loosened and softly dry like soil at the end of a sunny day. The young woman was wide-eyed. She could not have predicted that contentment was going to look so scuffed on the face of a woman.

I went to college in the early nineties. President George Bush, the first one, was in office, continuing in Ronald Reagan's tradition of "compassionate conservatism." Terms like "latchkey kid" and "right to life" and "family values" were common in the community where I grew up. The country wasn't as polarized then.

Reagan had been elected president in a landslide. I think even my father voted for him.

I wore long flowy skirts and ate square slices of pizza from a place called Pinocchio's. I watched *Beverly Hills 90210* and pined for the roguish Dylan. I still slept with the teddy bear that followed me from boarding school to college, but I also stayed out late at the college's all-male private clubs and drank beer or did shots. I didn't call myself a feminist when I arrived on campus, because I thought all feminists hated men. Feminists, the idea of them at least, made my stomach tingle with something that felt like fear. To be liked by others was the most important thing to me at that age. And feminists struck me as difficult to like because they were angry all the time. I did not want to be like that—angry all the time.

Midway through my sophomore year, my application to an Honors major was rejected because the department chair didn't think I had the chops to complete the coursework. This was late in the process of committing to an area of study, so I had to pivot quickly. My favorite class up until then had been American Women's history taught by Ellen Fitzpatrick. *A Midwife's Tale*, one of the books she assigned in that class, captivated me. It was a scholarly book based on the diaries of a midwife who lived and worked in the years following the American Revolution. The collection of letters and the historian's insightful interpretation of them revealed a version of American history I had never encountered in textbooks. I met people who reminded me of myself. I dipped into a historical record that provided concrete evidence of a narrative about colonial America that had been passed over in favor of the riots and battles that had been led by men. This book connected my own experience as a woman to that of another woman who had lived in the past. I loved the process of peeking behind the famous scenes of history at a private story, full of intimate detail, the way that so much could be gleaned about the time period, even though it was just one person's story. Since I was being forced to change plans at the last minute, switching to Women's Studies felt like an easy choice. I loved the material, and I liked that it was a tiny department with about twenty students and a small handful of professors. What I initially perceived as bad luck connected me to a close-knit scholarly community at an otherwise overwhelming university.

Professor Fitzpatrick's class and many of the books she taught made the argument that male doctors and western medicine had not always been the central health resource for American women. We studied the way that the founding of the American Medical Association in 1847 eroded the roles that midwives had played in local communities, a course of events that did not always lead to positive health outcomes for American women. The complicated relationship between American women's history and the history of medicine in the United States became the core theme of my undergraduate studies. For my thesis I wrote about the deployment of the birth control pill in the late sixties and a group of feminists who protested the process. They were in favor of birth control but had discovered that the hormone dosage in the first version of the pill was too high and caused fatal embolisms in some women. Their advocacy contributed to the development of a safer pill, more like the one women take today.

During my last two years of college, I disappeared for hours in the Schlesinger Library, working on my thesis research. In theory classes I chewed on texts that were challenging—works by Lacan and Foucault and Derrida. Sometimes after reading a difficult postmodern passage, my brain felt so hot with thinking I had to lay my head on my desk. I remember leaving a theory class one night with a headache, a brain spot behind my eye that squeezed like a fist. I walked into the New England night and my limbs jangled in their sockets. I felt like parts, two ankles, a stack of ribs, thick stick femurs, loose teeth in a hollow skull. My soft organs like birds perched on thin branches.

Recalling this young woman, my middle-aged-self wanted to wrap my arms around her. My college course work had taught me to deconstruct ideas about gender, an intellectual journey that forced me to sort through my own attitudes and behavior. Feminism asked me to consider which aspects of my personality were genuine to me and which were part of a gender performance that American girlhood had taught me to enact. While the answer wasn't always clear, even then I understood the value in the review. But the epistemological revision was destabilizing and often left me feeling unprotected, vulnerable in a way that was amplified by my parents' divorce and the way it had turned my home life upside down.

When I wasn't at school, I took on the role of the eldest daughter in a household headed by a single woman. I watched my younger brother while your grandmother (Nonny, my mom, not Dad's) worked. I fed us and organized our schedules. It was not uncommon for me to pack him up and drive him home from boarding school or drive him to summer camp even. Sometimes when Nonny had to travel, I was in charge of the two of us. During those times, I often had to argue with my father to use his car. My mother could not give hers up and my father lived in New York City, and the two of them could not talk to each other long or civilly enough to make a plan. When I needed a new computer for college, my mother could not afford it and sent me to my father to see if he would chip in. He refused and said she should pay for it out of child support. They would go back and forth like this for months on anything from clothes to bicycles to the cost of a session with a therapist.

The most difficult encounter I had with my family during these years took place on a hot summer afternoon in Grand Central Station. My father had just moved to New York City, and we were having lunch in a cafe. My father spent most of the meal weeping. I sat there under the station's vaulted blue ceiling and tried to distract myself by counting the tiny gold specks of stars painted into the blue dome of sky. Before dessert came, he told me I reminded him too much of my mother to keep seeing me. He needed to take a break—from me. Staring up at those gold stars, I felt a cold gust swoosh through me. My body went vacant, and I wondered how much longer I had to endure the lunch. I don't remember the lunch ending or how we said goodbye, just the exquisite sensation of vanishing. Sound roared in my ears while my body sat empty and still, like a shell. I didn't see my father for a long time after that. I don't know how much time passed, but in my recollection the span was vast. It was an epoch, an era in which selves died and were reborn. I learned how to earn my own money, I memorized the major highways and byways of New England, I applied for and was offered a grant for my undergraduate research. And perhaps, to prove to myself that I could do more than survive, I graduated in the top 10 percent of my Harvard class. I was so afraid of my own anger and so afraid of the fear itself that there was no way I could have expressed it then. Instead, I channeled an unimaginable amount of energy into my work. In the shadows of my life, I indulged in silent invisible acts of rage. Even though I earned my own spending money, I stole my father's credit card and used it to buy a printer, a pair of shoes, a hunk of expensive cheese. I did these things out of spite, propelled by the idea that he should have been paying for these things anyway.

Two days before graduation I received a notice that the university would not be giving me my diploma on graduation day. My tuition bill for the semester had not been paid, the money likely trapped in yet another argument between my parents. I imagined the humiliation I would feel when my grandfather asked to see my diploma after I walked down from the dais, and all I had to show for myself was an empty folio. I had worked too hard for that moment for it to be taken from me by my parents' divorce. So, I went to the registrar's office the next day, and when the gentleman behind the counter told me my enormous balance, I knew my parents would not be able to pay it before graduation. In a split second, without any awareness of what I was doing, I slipped into the best script I knew for persuading this gentleman to give me what I had earned. I cried. A particular kind of cry. One in which I allowed myself to appear powerless so that his own sense of power might be amplified by his ability to help me. He put his signature on my bill and assured me my diploma would be there at graduation.

Standing in the Radcliffe yard 25 years later, I recalled wishing I had had an adult who would go to bat for me back then. My parents were occupied by the enormous challenges in their own lives, and I was afraid to speak out on my own behalf. The combination left me on my own. My college self would have wanted things to be different for her. She would have wanted to be accepted to the area of study she preferred. She would have wanted her parents to stay together. She would have wanted more financial cushion than she had. But the snug courtyard of Radcliffe yard had fortified her and taught her to stand on her own. My college-self had no idea how much she was doing to prepare for the life that lay ahead. When she first walked through the gates of Radcliffe yard, she had no way of knowing she would give birth to three children who would be assigned female when they were born. She had no way of predicting how her study of gender would shape her family's future.

When you were in first grade and a clinician suggested that you might have gender dysphoria, my scholarly habits returned like muscle memory. Trained to regard interpretations of facts critically and to value primary sources above others, I purchased a subscription to the DSM, the American Psychiatric Association's diagnostic handbook (officially entitled *The Diagnostic and Statistical Manual of Mental Disorders*), so I could read the diagnosis myself. The fifth edition had just been published and gender dysphoria was one of the featured updates. The new diagnosis replaced gender identity disorder to de-pathologize gender diversity.

The first time I read it I felt like a Women's Studies student again. Stereotypes and gendered assumptions leapt from the text; eyesores that made me feel as if I were reading a document from another decade. Diagnoses I had studied as a college student came to mind. I remembered a passage about hysteria from the *New England Journal of Medicine* that I had used in a college paper. "Hysteria is ordinarily, but not without exception, a disease pertaining to the female organization...exclusively confined to the period of life during which the menstrual function is normally active: a much greater number of cases occur in the condition of virginity."* It was the way gender stereotype was elevated by authoritative

* *The New England Journal of Medicine* (1853) "Hysteria." 49, 1, 17–18. www.nejm.org/doi/full/10.1056/NEJM185308030490105

language that had stood out to me then and jumped out at me again when I read the clinical criteria for gender dysphoria in the DSM.

According to the DSM-5, gender dysphoria is a notable mismatch between the gender a person experiences and what was assigned to them at birth, for at least six months.*

Sitting with the text of the diagnosis the first time I read it, I checked off the "symptoms" you appeared to have. I recognized five, but they were hardly personality traits I felt comfortable calling symptoms. Preference for masculine clothes, preference for playmates of a particular gender, preference for rough-and-tumble play—all these pieces of "evidence" were so laden with stereotypical assumptions it was difficult to imagine using the information as "data" for a diagnosis. I was particularly disturbed by the term "cross-dressing" in association with little boys. It sounded unnecessarily homophobic and sexualizing. It stigmatized little boys who experimented with gender play in a way that it did not stigmatize girls who were experimenting with the same. This was exactly the kind of material I had been trained to read critically, and most of it was easily distilled into cultural assumptions about what it meant to be male and female. All kinds of feminist alarms sounded in my mind. The idea that this flawed psychological instrument would be used to recommend medical treatment for your gender struck me as patently absurd. I remember showing Dad my research. I dropped a bunch of f-bombs and told him that the diagnosis sounded to me like Dick and Jane fan fiction.

Of course, we eventually came to understand gender dysphoria

* For more information on this, see https://www.psychiatry.org/patients-families/gender-dysphoria/what-is-gender-dysphoria

as an embodied experience. We saw it emerge in front of our own eyes. I came to recognize it in you and in others. I eventually felt like I "got it" in a way that would not have been considered rigorous on the campus where I studied so hard. It was a kind of knowing that emerged in patterns. In sequences I witnessed in you and then heard about from other mothers, like the one in which a child refused to get in the pool in a boy's bathing suit, but when the mother had offered a girl's bathing suit, the child jumped right in. It was intuitive and felt like a buzz or a ripple when I watched you play, when I listened to you tell me about dreams in which you appeared as a boy, or when I heard you envisioning yourself as an adult man riding a bike. Clothes and stereotypes were part of the pattern, but they eventually spoke to me differently than they did when I first read the gender dysphoria diagnosis. I came to see them as a loose language or set of signals to help telegraph a way to see or be seen. Clothes were not just clothes for people with gender dysphoria; they were a kind of poetry, they were an echo, they pointed toward, but were not, and did not even stand for, the thing itself. They were an assertion and the beginning of a negotiation.

Returning to Harvard I saw that college was a chapter in my life that resonated far beyond the time I spent in Cambridge. Perhaps this was the reason people went to reunions. Over the weekend I stayed in a dorm with a group of women that had been organized by my friend. And even though I had not kept in touch with a lot of my classmates, by the end of the weekend many of these women felt like good friends, maybe better friends than we could have been to each other when we were 18. I hadn't expected to feel this way, but staying up late talking, sleeping in a freshmen dorm, eating in the Commons, I felt a part of something, part of a community that mattered to me. We were a group of women who were smart and hard working. Writers and therapists. Lawyers and doctors. Heads of nonprofits. One was a professor of human rights; another was a painter. A good number were full-time parents. One classmate I met over the weekend was a writer and also had a trans son about your age. We only spoke briefly because the context was so public, but she had a new book coming out and we agreed I'd interview her about it. I got so much out of being at my reunion, but if the only thing that had come out of it was meeting a smart mom who I can talk to about these big decisions we are facing—the trip would have been totally worth it.

REFLECTION QUESTIONS

- As an adult, what experiences can you remember that were formative in thinking of yourself as a boy or a girl? Can you recall an experience of deeply knowing you were a girl or a boy? Can you recall moments of feeling really happy, or alternatively unhappy, that you were a girl or a boy? Have you ever wondered what it would be like if you were born a different gender?
- Many adults living today grew up assuming that gender identity could be assumed based on the genitals a person was born with (or perceived to be born with). In what ways does your experience of your own gender fit into cultural assumptions? In what ways does it differ? Assuming you, yourself, do not have gender dysphoria, how do you understand that experience to be different from your own experience of gender alignment?

- How is raising your child forcing you to revise your ideas about gender? How confident do you feel about these changes? What resources have helped? If you feel like you need more support understanding gender dysphoria, where will you turn to learn more?

Letter 6
June 2019: Bringing a Daisy to a Gunfight

Issues continued to come up at school from time to time. Among other choice proclamations, one boy had declared that inclusion statements were for the weak-minded. His mom called me that day. She had been one of a small group of parents we knew before you started at your new school. She had attended a parent ed event about gender that we had hosted, so when she heard about what her son had been up to at school, she called to find out how you were doing and to apologize for the kinds of things he had been saying. Like many moms of boys your age, she was fighting against a tide of homophobic and anti-trans rhetoric that her son was encountering online. She didn't know what to do but was determined to get him to a better place. She told me that she was going to send him to the public library to read about dangers the LGBTQIA+ community faced. She was so supportive and assured me that she would not talk to her son about your gender history. I believed her, and I was also very nervous. It felt like your privacy was being maintained by the thinnest thread. It would take so little for someone to find out about your gender history and then announce it to the whole school.

If that weren't stressful enough, during the same week the

Department of Health and Human Services proposed a new rule to roll back healthcare protections for the trans community. When I read the headline my heart raced; my skin felt like it was being pricked by tiny electric needles. Headlines had never had a physical impact on me before. Even when abortion rights came under threat, I had always known that somehow, some way, I could get to the resources I needed. But the notion that you might be denied access to medical care, that something could happen to me, and you would be on your own in a hostile culture eager to deny you basic everyday medical needs, filled me with a new kind of terror. I had never felt so afraid of new legislation. It had never ever felt so personal.

I knew I was not the first mother to feel this way. I was joining legions of mothers—Black mothers, mothers of disabled children, mothers of soldiers and veterans, poor mothers—who knew this feeling all too well. And even though I'd been aware of my own privilege, my understanding had been theoretical. During the Trump administration, though, I was experiencing firsthand the day-to-day stress of living under constant public threat. Fear for your bodily safety became the constant backdrop of my days. Cynicism became my defense against the pain of having to explain the same particularities of your needs over and over and over again, and I had the impression that people who never had to contend with such a threatening context walked around in their own clueless fiction most of the time. And this was with all the education, financial and class advantages that I knew our family had. We were far safer than most families who lived in the margins of American culture, and still I was afraid. I was afraid every day.

The newness of my own fear showed my previous "can-do" optimism in a dark light. For most of my life I had assumed I belonged in the classrooms and offices and homes I walked into. I had a kind of shiny confidence that led me to believe I could count on things working out most of the time. I thought everyone did. I didn't worry about missing a bill payment, speeding on the highway, or touching things in a department store. When I was a college student and cried at the university registrar's office about my unpaid tuition, an exception was made. Thinking about who I used to be before parenting a trans child during the Trump administration felt like looking at a picture of myself as a child. That girl was sweet. I still felt fondly toward her, but there was so much suffering she could not imagine. It was hard not to feel pissed off at her for all that she failed to comprehend.

As soon as Trump took office, protections for the trans community started to disappear. When the Department of Education rolled back Obama's executive order that recognized discrimination against gender identity as sex discrimination, I was startled, but I didn't feel fear in my body. I thought our progressive community would protect us from Trump's bigotry. But after all we had been through—after losing local friendships, after being let down by your previous school, after having had to move homes and schools and change your name, all so you could fly a little more under the radar—I no longer felt assured by where we lived. And while you are better protected by the laws in California than you would be in other parts of the country, this does not change the fact that this administration has endangered you every day. Every time Trump made an announcement that rolled back protections for the trans community, a new round of anti-trans bigotry erupted.

These fears were constant—they even jangled me in my sleep. I dreamt of black uniformed soldiers pointing their machine guns at us. I dreamt of being stuck on a prison ship from which we could not escape. I dreamt we were hidden in a basement. In the early evenings I poured myself a drink more often. Many times a day I found myself standing at the counter putting a corner of someone else's leftover toast or a cookie or mac'n'cheese into my mouth. When the salty, chewy macaroni met my bite, or when the chocolate chip from the cookie melted on my tongue, when the corner of toast turned to velvet in the cave of my mouth, when the heat of the bourbon softened the inside of my skull, I felt relaxed. For a flash I tricked my body into remembering safety. The sensation felt like having my head cradled in my mother's lap, her hand stroking my hair, but it did not last. Sometimes it was less than a breath long. But when the news was bad, that fraction of a breath was the easiest part of my day.

And there you were yesterday—baking. The smell of sugar made our kitchen feel so cozy. Flour dusted the counter where you had laid out a square of plastic wrap. You were mixing different food dyes into white icing. I watched as you piped a stripe of each new color onto the plastic wrap. Then you rolled them all together and squeezed the assortment through a pastry bag onto a fresh-baked cupcake. A rainbow swirl of frosting spiraled into a colorful peak. When you looked up from your work, you told me about a plan you had to deliver cupcakes to our neighbors along with messages directing them to a website site you were making. Your goal was to raise awareness about issues facing LGBTQIA+ kids. You said, "Mom, who wouldn't like a rainbow cupcake?" And it was like a stone had lodged in my chest. I pulled you in for a hug.

In my house you've learned how to bake, how to draw, how to invite people to a party, but near nothing about how to manage discrimination. Is it right for you to hand a cupcake to someone who doesn't respect your identity? Am I supposed to encourage you to be friendly and civil to people like that, or am I supposed to warn you against them? The fact is, I didn't know in that moment, and I don't know now, how to keep a trans child safe. Even with my Women's Studies background, I don't know how to fight institutional oppression, not really. I don't know how to demand healthcare when the gender marker on your insurance card might cause you to be denied care you needed. Not only have I not taught you these things, but I'm also afraid I've failed to teach you to prioritize your self-protection. Sometimes it feels like I've handed you a daisy for a gunfight.

REFLECTION QUESTIONS

- Think of a time you have had to advocate for yourself. What were your strategies? What personal strengths and values did you lean into to make your voice heard? How could you use your own experiences of self-advocacy to talk to your child about keeping safe?
- Who do you rely on in your community to help keep your child mentally and physically safe? What skills or information do these allies need to help sustain your child's wellbeing?
- If you have questions about how to keep your child safe in your community, whom can you turn to? Who has proven themselves to be supportive and informed? How do you stay connected to this person or team? How can you empower your child to connect with this person or team if they feel afraid and you are not available?

Letter 7

June 2019: The Right to Reproduce

I scheduled an appointment with Dr. Henderson, the psychologist we met at that first gender clinic, because I wanted to talk to someone about what fertility meant to trans people. Her ability to pair the clinical process with genuine understanding about the emotional depths of your experience had impressed me, even on that very first day when I had been processing so much. Also, Dr. Henderson was the only trans adult I was aware of knowing. She was the one and only person I could think of who might be able to share a first-person perspective about what fertility meant to trans adults.

Her office was in Rockridge, an Oakland neighborhood I loved because of how different it was from where we lived. If Silicon Valley was Teslas and office buildings and cell phone stores, Oakland was the East Bay Depot for Creative Reuse, an organization that keeps materials out of landfill and redistributes them as free art supplies for schools, and the East Bay Queer Arts Center, and the Market Hall Food Court, a grocery store where I once bought the best sandwich I ever ate—buffalo mozzarella and tomato on olive bread seasoned with basil and bits of preserved lemon. Walking around the neighborhood before the appointment made me feel like the trip to see Dr. Henderson would be worthwhile.

I arrived in her waiting room early. She entered the room through the elevator, and the breeze from the elevator's motion skimmed her blonde bangs off her forehead. As she welcomed me into her office, she explained that she had been teaching a class that had run a few minutes late. Her office was shaped like the prow of a ship. Golden views of the Oakland hills surrounded us, and late afternoon sun poured through the window. Bright squares of light danced on the floor.

Dr. Henderson wore a bulky sweater that had been knit with delicate textured yarn. Horned buttons accented the sweater's seam, and a wide collar spread like elephant ears on her shoulders. The scale of the sweater was large, but its details were soft and organic. A necklace of brown beads the size of plums laid across her collar bone and peeked through the "v" of her blouse. A pair of studious tortoise shell glasses framed her face. She was beautiful. Although what struck me more viscerally was how her smile, the way it softened and creased her face, made me feel comfortable in her space.

I spent the first part of the appointment bringing her up to speed on our journey. "Gender isn't what I thought it was," I told her, and then added, "I thought I had thought about it a lot too." She laughed, throwing her head back, as if to say, *Welcome to the party of this paradox*. Then she said something that stuck with me. She told me she had been thinking about the definition of gender for a long time, and that the phrase she was about to share with me was the best she had come up with so far: "Gender is nature through nurture in culture." In my mind I saw a set of gears, and when the gear of nature turned, it moved the gear of nurture and culture. Any of the individual wheels had the ability to turn the other two. As culture became more open, families would nurture differently. More of nature might find the opportunity to be expressed. If nurturing was rigid, differences in nature and differences in culture might become more difficult to express. Even though I had studied gender for years, until she said this, my mental model had been inert. I had thought of gender (whether male or female or some expression of a spectrum) as a label for describing people. Dr. Henderson's description was dynamic. It accounted for different aspects of lived experience impacting each other. She described a process that encompassed the kinds of negotiations or trade-offs an individual might make based on the context in which they lived.

We talked about the gender dysphoria diagnosis. She described how she worked with it in her practice despite its shortcomings. "Science likes to measure and categorize things in order to make predictions," she told me. Her take was that the gender dysphoria diagnosis reflected this tradition but did not capture the whole experience. She told me a little of her personal story, and then said, "There was a time I didn't have gender dysphoria, then I had it, and now I don't, but any psychiatrist would tell you that I do have it in order to get my treatments," as if gender dysphoria was both a description of a person's state as well a tool for negotiation within the culture. So even if a person was not in a state of distress because of their gender, the diagnosis might still apply to them if their gender identity required hormone therapy.

I explained to her that until we met her at the gender clinic in San Francisco, our whole family called your gender "middle." I told her about our trip to Hawaii and about the article I had read on the flight home about a master hula dancer who identified as *māhū*, the ancient Hawaiian word for a gender not male or female, but in-between. Sitting in her office, I thought about how that aspect of Hawaiian culture reinforced my own idea that gender could be experienced as a spectrum, and how in our case nurture and culture both opened a window for you. But for a few years these same influences also created limits around the medical steps I was willing to take on behalf of your gender. If there really was a middle, a version of gender that was not either/or, did we need to force bodies onto a masculine or feminine path? I loved telling her that when I explained to you that there was a middle gender in Hawaii, you asked me, "Can we have middle in California?"

Sharing this story with her, I already felt nostalgic for middle gender. I loved those years we spent skirting language, watching you upend other people's expectations. Back then I thought your life was proving that gender was over, that people could be whatever they wanted. I had been trained to understand gender as a social construct, a set of expectations that culture wielded to assign people roles, and you were blowing right through expectations that people had for girls. It went against everything I had learned to believe that your drive to roughhouse or play with boys had an innate component. But we went to the gender clinic for the first time, because I had started to surrender to the idea that your gender expression was rooted in something real and true in your body. How it was rooted in your body, I didn't know, but I felt it strongly enough that I thought it was appropriate to seek medical treatment.

Since then, I had exhausted myself trying to square what I saw in you with what I not only had learned about gender in culture but had also experienced myself. My life had taught me firsthand that gender was shaped by social expectations. And yet, your masculinity had been clear to me before it was possible for you to have had any social understanding at all. With the help of Dr. Henderson's definition, I realized both insights could be true without one negating or diluting the other. Releasing the conflict between them felt like putting down a sack of bricks I had been carrying for years.

It meant that our family's idea of middle had maybe been true for a while but wasn't the whole story. I wondered aloud if it had been folly to let a Hawaiian idea about gender influence your childhood in Silicon Valley. The next thing I knew I was crying, asking Dr. Henderson, "Do you think I did okay? I mean, did I do all right?" as the uncertainty I'd had over the last eight years poured out of me. Dr. Henderson sat quietly with me as I cried. After a bit, I looked up and saw her gaze out the window before saying to me, "Your son is lucky." Her affirmation made me feel that my doubts and our family's inventions had their place. I could be completely behind you and still feel confused. We could use our own language to describe your gender and still be naming your truth. If we were learning anything at all, it was that the sturdiest thinking about gender had the capacity to hold an idea both ways.

When I asked her about trans adults and parenting, she told me that her own children were born before she transitioned. I got the impression that she was happy to have had children, but that the hurdles she surmounted to achieve gender congruence were less related to fertility than yours have been, and that her journey through the landscape of gender had taken her across different territory than the terrain we are traveling. Later in the conversation, she told me about a recent ride she took on BART

(Bay Area Rapid Transit), the local public transportation, when a fellow rider took a swing at her. It was a potent reminder that life as a trans woman, even in the most progressive part of the USA, was still dangerous. Even though I worried about your safety every day, I knew you didn't face the same kinds of threats trans women did, and especially that trans women of color did. We were lucky that our main preoccupation had to do with your fertility. Lots of trans people, kids and adults alike, had more fundamental challenges taking up their time and resources.

Before I left her office, Dr. Henderson told me about a community of trans people living in Sweden. In the nineteen-nineties, the Swedish government required surgical sterilization as part of legal gender affirmation, which meant that to get a driver's license or passport or medical benefits that aligned with their gender identity, Swedish citizens had to agree to surgically sterilize themselves. Years later, believing that this requirement violated their human rights, they petitioned the Swedish government to pay reparations. And they won. This story affirmed my thought that the reproductive rights of trans people were important, that my urgency around exploring your options was not a version of cis bias, and the instinct that trans kids' reproductive futures deserved deep consideration was neither unfounded nor unprecedented.

When Dr. Henderson stood next to the door of her office as I walked out, her stature reminded me of the ancient stone-carved maidens that guarded the Erechtheion in Athens; she carried their same grace and substance and strength. I left feeling grounded and energized. Her dynamic description of gender, along with her genuine presence, convinced me further of your masculinity. Not only were you a boy—you were a boy growing up in California in the early twenty-first century. Affirming gender with hormone therapy is the best treatment available during the cultural moment in which we are living. This is not something I can or want to change. Realizing this, I knew for sure we would do the testosterone shots. I felt the yoke between your identity and your fertility loosen. I was no longer torn between one and the other. There was no choice about it. You were a transgender boy who would experience a testosterone puberty.

At the same time, your fertility was important. The Swedish trans community had confirmed (again—how many times must this be proven?) that reproductive rights were human rights. For trans kids like you, this is a knot that still needs untangling. I don't know if our family will be able to solve the puzzle, but my meeting with Dr. Henderson convinced me that we should try. Walking back to my car, I indulged in revisiting my vision of your future self. There he was, a grown man, holding the hand of a little boy. I knew the man, but who was that little boy? How did he belong to you? Was it possible that he might be more than a metaphor?

REFLECTION QUESTIONS

- Each child's gender journey is unique and will generate unique medical concerns. What medical questions are surfacing in your family?
- How is your family handling mental health support as well as medical support? What resources might you connect with to feel that your family's mental health is well supported? What support are you receiving? What do you need? If your child has accompanying conditions

like ADHD, autism, anxiety or depression, how is your child being supported at home and at school?

- Who in your community can connect you with supportive medical professionals? If you don't know who that would be, what organization or community might you turn to for a referral?
- Have you asked your child's physician about a long-term medical timeline? Are there surgeries that need to be scheduled? Do you need referrals to other specialists?
- What is the impact of financial concerns? Who can help you understand, for sure, what medical support your insurance will or won't cover? Where might you find out about grants to help pay for procedures your child might need?

Interview

Chase Strangio on the Reproductive Trans Body

Chase Strangio is Deputy Director for Transgender Justice with the American Civil Liberties Union's (ACLU) Lesbian, Gay, Bisexual, Transgender, Queer (LGBT) and HIV Project and a nationally recognized expert on transgender rights. Chase's work includes impact litigation, as well as legislative and administrative advocacy, on behalf of LGBTQ people and people living with HIV across the USA.

Prior to joining the ACLU, Chase was an Equal Justice Works fellow and Director of Prisoner Justice Initiatives at the Sylvia Rivera Law Project, where he represented transgender and gender nonconforming individuals in confinement settings. In 2012, Chase co-founded the Lorena Borjas Community Fund, an organization that provides direct bail/bond assistance to LGBTQ immigrants in criminal and immigration cases. Chase is a graduate of Northeastern University School of Law and Grinnell College.

Chase has served as counsel in the ACLU's challenge to North Carolina's notorious HB2,* *Carcaño, et al. v. Cooper, et al.*,† the

* The Public Facilities Privacy & Security Act, commonly known as House Bill 2 or HB2.

† www.aclu.org/cases/carcano-et-al-v-cooper-et-al

ACLU's challenge to Trump's trans military ban, *Stone v. Trump*,* and the case of *R.G. & G.R. Harris Funeral Homes v. EEOC & Aimee Stephens*,† which was heard by the Supreme Court in October 2019.

Cristina: For parents who are raising trans kids in the middle of the current political backlash, what would you share about the reproductive trans body, family building, and parenting in a trans life? Part of me doesn't even want to ask that question. It feels biased to ask about it, because, of course, like all people, trans people will and won't want to build families. But I want to ask about it because I think there is a bias against trans folks who want to become parents. And I'm just curious what you would want parents of trans kids to know about or think about as they're stewarding their children into the future.

Chase: What's funny is that like everything with our opponents, there's such a hypocrisy to the context, because on the one hand, it's like they don't want us to be parents and on the other, they're using our potential future fertility as the basis for denial of care as if they want to foster that fertility in the future.

In the same way they are also arguing against top surgery by saying we must ensure that people can breastfeed. As if that's the primary state interest in stopping trans top surgery. First, as a society, we do nothing to support and cultivate breastfeeding. So, let's just stop right there, right? Second, lots of people don't, or can't, breastfeed or chest feed for a multitude of reasons, depending on who the person is. And so, everything is disingenuous

* www.aclu.org/cases/stone-v-trump

† www.aclu.org/cases/rg-gr-harris-funeral-homes-v-eeoc-aimee-stephens

when it comes to trying to restrict people's ability to realize their full potential. Ultimately, if the state really cared about those things—preserving fertility for trans young people or preserving options for more choices around family formation—there's a million ways to invest in that. For example, expanding research into fertility, expanding access to fertility preservation, supporting people making choices about their families and caring for their families, which, by the way, we don't help people do at all. And so, I think first and foremost all the bias against trans fertility is so disingenuous, but it's so real at the same time.

And when it comes to how we support parents who are supporting their trans kids, especially in this pandemic moment, we have to acknowledge there's so much we don't know about what's going to happen to our kids in the future. Plus the fact that becoming a parent is such a leap of faith. Essentially, we need to try to create as much care and support and options for the future as we can. But the future itself is feeling so precarious. I hope my kids live on a planet that's hospitable enough to have a family. We are all contending with a lot of questions about the future, and what it will mean to conceive children and raise families and an increasingly precarious world that we're living in.

I think everything needs to be placed in that perspective. We don't know what's going to be available for our children and so, first and foremost, we should help protect them and support them in the moment. And a part of that, of course, is planning for what they may be able to do in the future. And I do know trans people who feel sad that they didn't take fertility preservation options. Especially people who could have. Everyone I know—I'm 39, no one I know had access to puberty blockers—which means before any reduced fertility, people could have had the option and just weren't told about that. And so, I think part of that regret, for many people in my generation, is not so much I wasn't old enough to make the decision; I just regret that no one told me what was available to me. So, I think a lot of it is getting to the bottom of what's actually true, and what's actually possible, and making sure that our children, our peers, and everyone is informed about those things, and then supported in the financial cost of it all, because obviously fertility preservation and the storage of eggs and sperm is expensive.

And what does it mean to provide that support in our community? And to prioritize the possibility for trans people to biologically reproduce if that's what they want to do? It's about creating the possibility and not letting the idea that people may be adamantly opposed to it get in the way. It is, of course, complicated with minors. Minors, obviously, have some level of different judgment than people do as adults. And something you believe very strongly when you're younger may not be true when you're older. It's also true that for many people, they know exactly what they want. And that remains true throughout their whole life; the way our brain processes it or expresses it may change, but some people know very strongly certain things about themselves that remain true throughout a lifetime. And I think it's just a matter of balancing who our kids are. We also have to trust our kids and their agency and support that while supporting their future agency as well. Given the current moment that we're living in and the culture that we're living in, advocating for a child's potential for future family building is part of deeply acknowledging who they are. That is seeing trans kids as whole people. And that's an important part of having these deeper, more nuanced conversations and explorations about giving trans kids the same access to care and opportunity as other children, such as the options pediatric cancer patients receive.

Cristina: What is your vision for the future of trans rights? Where do you find hope, and how do you think about it?

Chase: I'll start with how I find hope because I think that's what moves us forward. I find hope in the fact that no matter how many anti-trans laws they pass, no matter how many ways that we start to see these various forms of backlash, we'll never lose the reality that more and more people are feeling comfortable with who they are, more and more people are living their truth, and more and more people are pushing back on our understanding of what was even possible about gender. That forward momentum is continuing to move forward.

Every generation experiences a new possibility for self-actualization that wasn't available to the prior generation. And we see it even in five-year increments. For example, I had top surgery in 2009. I have friends who are having top surgery now, and it's already a different world. In terms of both access—I had to fly across the country and stay at a hotel that I booked on Priceline; there was no Airbnb, and there was no insurance coverage, I used my student loans—and now people are staying in their hometowns. There are surgeons who provide gender-affirming care in their own communities. Lots of people are covered by insurance. And in a decade, you can see how much has changed. And obviously, access to affirming care, in particular affirming surgical care, is still very much out of reach for many people, far too many people. But it's been transformed.

And even as states try to restrict our access, the truth and momentum of our existence, and the continued experiencing and realizing of who we can be as individuals, is growing. And so, the future I'm imagining is one where that just continues to grow, and we have more and more opportunities to learn about what's possible for us as individuals, and where we continue to engage everyone, not just trans people, not just nonbinary people, in understanding that we're all a part of systems of gender. The more people feel both implicated and affected, the more engaged they will become, because ultimately, the more the states act to restrict the possibilities for us to realize who we are, the more it hurts everyone. I imagine a future where gender is both more and less salient. It's more salient in that we can celebrate all of the things that make us who we are. And less salient in that we don't organize society around gender binary that isn't serving us. And I think that will ultimately make for a more beautiful set of possibilities for everyone.

Letter 8

July 2019: The Cost of Safety

The office for the ACLU of Northern California is in a humble block in downtown San Francisco—the entrance is next to a convenience store. The day I visited, trash littered the sidewalk, and a single black boot lay on its side near the curb. As I waited for someone to buzz me in, I stared at the Transamerica building with its pointed crown. When I moved to the Bay Area in the nineties, it was the highest building in the city. It had recently been dwarfed by the Salesforce Tower, the building that has a giant movie screen wrapped around its top floors. Patches of the city were dirtier than they had ever been. Some blocks were cluttered with smashed cans, edges of food in wrappers, and dark smears that were both mysterious and grotesque. Rows of tents and makeshift shelters cobbled together out of old blankets and sleeping bags crowded many of the sidewalks. Meanwhile, gentrified blocks with luxury condos and brand-new storefronts appeared just across the street. Twenty years ago, San Francisco did not look like this. The city had become a tableau of who counted and who didn't. Standing outside the ACLU office, it chilled me to recall that nearly half of the homeless youth in the city were part of the LGBTQ+ community.

After I was buzzed in, an elevator dropped me off in a clean, modern reception area with a sign that indicated I was at the ACLU. A receptionist led me to a conference room, where I met with Elizabeth Gill and a development officer named Shernaz. Shernaz offered me a bottle of sparkling water and asked about you and your sisters. I didn't feel like talking about you right then. I wanted to hear from Elizabeth, to learn what concerned her most, and to better understand whether my own fears about your public life were rational or not.

An attorney with short professional hair who wore a dark-colored blazer, Elizabeth Gill was a senior staff attorney who led litigation and advocacy for the LGBTQ+ community. One case she shared with me was Oliver Knight's. Knight is a trans man living in Humboldt County, California. As part of Oliver Knight's gender-affirming care, he was scheduled to have a hysterectomy, but a few minutes before the procedure was to take place, the hospital called off his operation. At first, Knight couldn't get a straight answer from anyone about why the surgery had been cancelled. But when he finally asked his doctor if the administration had called it off was because he was transgender, the doctor had said simply, "Yes."

I was shocked. I had no idea a hospital could do something like that, just cancel a doctor's orders. Elizabeth explained that the hospital in Humboldt County is part of the Dignity Health network, a Catholic organization, and as such, they claimed that refusing care in this case was an issue of their organization's right to religious liberty.

I recognized the Dignity Health brand and asked if the organization operated in other California counties. Elizabeth told me that the company runs 39 hospitals, most of which are in

California. I was dumbfounded. It's hard to believe that at 39 different hospitals in California, a trans person's medical care is not guaranteed. I shook my head and asked her if I was understanding the case correctly. And she replied, "This is what our case is about."

As soon as I was alone in my car, I looked up Sequoia Hospital on my phone. It's the hospital closest to your school. Sure enough, it's part of the Dignity Health network. I had visited many friends who had babies there; Sequoia was known in our circle as the closest hospital that offered new mothers a private room. Dad and I knew it well. Or we thought we did. We had no idea it was part of a network of Catholic hospitals. That night I explained this to Dad. And asked him if he thought you would be safe being seen there in an emergency.

"I'm sure he'd be fine," Dad said calmly. In his mind there's no way that a hospital in Silicon Valley would refuse to treat you. This was one of the only topics around which Dad and I landed on different sides. I pointed out that we had moved and changed schools exactly because our assumptions about our community had been wrong. I felt exasperated. Normally I don't mind being the lead parent managing your care, and often, bringing Dad up to speed on a topic is a helpful way of processing new information. But telling him about my trip to the ACLU was underscoring how little control we had over your safety and care. The usual feeling of competence I had when I reported back to him was replaced by a heightened fear I felt about your life outside our home. I agreed that most people in our community were with us. But then I tried to make my point again, "It only takes one person, one single transphobic person..." My voice trailed off as I envisioned my newest nightmare: you wheeling up to Sequoia in an ambulance, and a faceless religious fanatic in the ER slowing down, or worse, denying your emergency treatment because treating a trans person offended their personal religious values.

"I just can't see that happening here," Dad said again.

"Well," I said, "I couldn't imagine a friend telling me that their son would never share a tent with ours. But it happened."

Dad sighed. We didn't say much after that, partly because it was too painful, and partly because neither of us really knows for sure whether Sequoia is safe for you. They could deny you care, but would a Silicon Valley hospital actually do that? And we don't know how to find out. After thinking about it for a couple of days, I decided it wasn't worth taking any chances. In the case of an emergency, I think you have to go to Stanford University Medical Center, even though it's a mile farther away from your school than Sequoia. Realizing this has been a turning point for me. It's one thing to deal with ignorant helicopter parents, but discrimination at hospitals is a problem of an entirely different scale—one that is well out of my control.

When I sat by your bedside that night and told you that if there was ever an accident and someone was taking you to the hospital that you had to tell them to take you to Stanford, I tried to say it with as little emotion as possible. But when you asked me why, I could barely open my mouth. Uttering, "I don't know if it's safe," was one of the worst things I have ever had to say to you. Your face did not register any emotion. You just turned on your side and mumbled, "Okay." I didn't know what to think. Was this an okay way of coping, to compartmentalize and process issues when you were ready? Did I deliver the information harshly? Were you afraid? Are you still? I thought of that black boot on the curb outside the ACLU office and the person whose foot should have been inside it. That person had fallen off some precipice, had crashed through whatever slim safety net Americans were supposed to have. Whatever limit existed between security and precarity had always felt far away from our lives. But after the conversation with Elizabeth Gill, that precipice felt closer than ever.

REFLECTION QUESTIONS

- What is your family's culture around emergency planning? Do you have a safety plan for a house fire or flooding? How have you helped your children process unexpected or scary events? How do you communicate that yes, bad things can happen, and you are a family who gets through hard things?
- Who can you talk to about creating a safety plan for your child? What aspects of your geography and living situation pose the most serious risk to your child?
- How aware is your child of these risks? What is your plan for talking to your child about this? Who else might help you do this in such a way that helps your child feel empowered rather than scared?

Letter 9

July 2019: A Boy Named Jane

You and I stayed in the car while we watched a camp counselor tumble your duffle bag into the back of a tractor and then drive away. By then I had memorized your packing list—one sleeping bag, eight pairs of shorts, eight shirts, three pairs of swim trunks, two flashlights, socks and boxer-briefs, an extra-long twin sheet, two bandanas, a tube of sunscreen, two 32 ounce water bottles, a spray can of insect repellent. Going through it again in my head had become a mantra of sorts, a way of controlling the only thing I could control during the week you'd spend at camp. I repeated the list to myself again and glanced over at you before getting out of the car. I watched you take a breath, then settle into your body before you pulled at the handle to open the door.

I had heard about Camp Aranu'tiq from a friend of mine on the East Coast who also had a trans son. He had attended camp for two summers, and she felt it strengthened their whole family for him to be part of a community of trans kids. I was happy when you decided to give it a try this summer. It seemed obvious to me that being in a community of peers would be good for you, but then you asked me why you didn't have a coming out story. We know this, that each trans person has a unique journey, but it had never occurred to me that yours would make you feel different than your trans peers. It had been such a relief during the school year (at least for most of the time) to be just another guy in your grade. You'd been able to relax into a boring obscurity that was still novel to you. When you asked me about having a coming out story, you forced me to rethink what joining a group of trans peers would mean to you. I had imagined an instant, shared connection, but on reflection, any group of people, no matter what element of shared experience they have, is always a group of individuals. Who knew what would happen at camp. You were probably right to assume that most of your fellow campers would have a coming out story that you didn't have, or at least that you didn't have yet.

Still, there had been a time in your past when we didn't know you'd been assigned the wrong gender. You did have a before and after, like other kids did. But once you cut your hair short, your gender was so fluid, so liminal, that it sometimes felt like magic. And that experience of living between genders, of being read one way by strangers and experienced in a different way by friends, was the part of your experience that felt more pronounced. The between-ness came naturally to you; from the looks of it, delighted you, actually. So, we invented the phrase "middle gender" as a way of naming your experience. Once I overheard you say to a gender therapist that your "middle years" gave you a lot of time to work on your gender identity. Until I heard you put it this way, I didn't realize that the joy of your gender play was a kind of work that helped you figure yourself out. Your gender was read fluidly by others for at least six years, and we didn't force anyone—you or the community around you—to coalesce around a fixed resolution. While this might have been confusing to other families, it was clear as day for our family. You were you. Your personality, your soul, your you-ness was unperturbed by conventional words or ideas that didn't fit you. There was no coming out, because by inventing middle gender, we stumbled into an idea that kept your unique self out in the open without taking on the problems associated with language and identification. If anything, our approach made it clear that you were not the problem, but that the trouble people had reading you originated in limited ideas that came from culture and language.

When you joined the rock-climbing team when you were about ten, one of your teammates asked if you were a boy or a girl. "What do you think?" you asked, putting the question back in his court. When he said he didn't know and badgered you to just tell him already, you told him you were fine with whichever and just kept climbing. When he said he needed to know, you told him that was his problem. You felt no need to manage his gender anxiety.

I felt so plucky about these kinds of stories. I felt so sure we were doing right by you (incidentally, if you ever decide to become a parent, that smug confidence is a sure sign that as a parent you are about to be humbled). That is, until the day I had to explain to you why we needed to rethink our approach. It was during sixth grade, a few days before you were going to visit your new school to see if it might be a fit for you. A mom friend of mine worked there. She was coordinating your visit, and when she called to ask me what the teachers and students should call you, I had no idea how to reply. I had been so preoccupied with the trouble we were having with some of the mothers at school and our upcoming move that I hadn't even considered this aspect of your visit. So that afternoon, when I had you in the car, I asked you how you wanted to be referred to at the new school. And you told me "He/him for sure." Then I asked you what name you wanted to use.

"I want to be a boy named Jane." I smiled, savoring for one of the last times the future we had allowed ourselves to imagine. I wanted you to be a boy named Jane, too. I should have told you more clearly that our family had invented language, had invented our own gender. I should have told you that it was unusual that we had not made you choose male or female. That you wanted to be a boy named Jane was my proudest and sorriest thing. I should have told you that we were at the beginning of things, and that the future, the way Dad and I imagined it was, like the author William Gibson wrote, "not equally distributed." I should have tried to explain that if pockets of gender progress existed, they were not promised. We didn't make it up exactly: nonbinary and transgender communities were hard at work making the future possible for you. It was happening all around us, just like the self-driving car, but like the self-driving car, it had not yet fully arrived. I should have told you that we were able to play at the edge of gender the way we did, at least in part, because we had the racial and economic privilege to afford the risk we were taking. We sent you to a small progressive private school; we lived in a town that considered itself tolerant. I thought our community believed in the same future. But I had been wrong—not wrong about everything, but wrong about enough things that you had no idea about the challenge that being a boy named Jane would pose. You chose the name Jake, because it was just one letter away from Jane, the name we gave you when you were born. The decision was quick and practical. We never for a minute considered that my cousin has a son your age also named Jake. I've often wondered if it annoyed their family that we chose the name, but I haven't ever asked about it. Every time I play out that conversation in my head, it just feels too complicated.

When we drove across town for your visiting day, I turned on the radio to distract us from our nerves. On the way, you asked me what you should do if you forgot to respond to the name Jake. "There's no way you're going to forget," I said, even though I worried I was wrong. It was like you were getting ready to walk on a stage for opening night. Would you remember your lines? Would the other kids go along with it? Would the adults remember what the plan was? What good would reinforcing your fears do? I was anxious in an unfamiliar way. And as I often did, I did everything I could to hide my concerns from you. Changing names, after having lived so happily with the name we gave you, felt like going into involuntary hiding, because other people would, with a simple switch of language, assume you had been using Jake and masculine pronouns your whole life. In the back of my mind, I knew that other people's assumptions about your gender might be experienced as deception if they ever learned your history. And their shock, the way it made people, mostly men, feel, was the primary reason that trans people—trans women of color, especially—are targets for violence.

I used to think coming out was something people did to express their authentic selves—a brave announcement staking a claim to a certain identity. But I had begun to understand coming out as having more to do with other people's assumptions about someone's identity rather than that individual's personal expression. The need for a person to come out as trans was a manifestation of how deeply conventions, language for one, carved gender into our cognition. A hairstyle was all it took for a child to invoke a cognitive legacy fashioned over many generations. When people came out, they were pushing against the weight of history. It was not so much a celebration as it was cultural labor that the LGBTQ+ community did on behalf of everyone else. You didn't have a typical coming out story to tell because you did not participate inside the convention of other people's ideas about gender for very long. You lived as "middle gender" for six years. When you arrived at summer camp you had only been living as a boy named Jake for a single school year, although you had been living as yourself for much, much longer than that. And since we've made it to the end of the school year without any further incidents, who knows how long it will be until you feel like sharing your history with people.

As we watched your duffle bag disappear down the dirt road to your cabin, I wondered what kind of coming out stories you'd hear at camp, and whether not having one was going to matter. This was just one of the questions I had. And I imagined you felt the same. But as we entered the camp dining hall to check you into your first ever week of summer camp, I felt myself zero in on a singular mission—to get you to your cabin and hug you goodbye without dissolving in a pool of tears. I had only known the camp's specific location for a week, because it was important to keep the camp address confidential for the safety of the campers. We also had to sign an agreement that we would not take pictures at camp for the same reason. All of this confidentiality was so different from my own experience of summer camp. But once we entered the dining hall, and the hot damp air clung to the back of my neck and the buzz of many voices meshed together filling the air around me, I felt the same anticipation and joy I recalled from my own summer camp days. The mess hall with its high rafters decorated with hand-painted banners that read, "Welcome!" "Be AWESOME" and "You BELONG HERE!" reminded me of how it felt to be a kid who belonged to a community that wasn't my family. The feeling encouraged me, even though I could see in the way you looked out from under your brow that you were still undecided. We wove our way through a maze of picnic tables, picked up your bunk assignment, and then stopped in front of a chair where you had to sit and have someone check your hair for lice.

While you were sitting still in the chair, I had a minute to look around. I saw a tall, lanky counselor with a brown ponytail and perfect eyebrows. I saw a camper with rainbow socks and hair that was tipped bright green. There was a tall, fit young man with brown skin and dark tattoos who I thought might be a counselor, and then a whole sea of kids who looked just like, well, just like a bunch of kids. A feeling of awe came over me then as I became aware of being in a room dominated by trans people. It was so rare for us, for you, to be in a group of people where you were one of many and I was one of only a few. As I took in the situation, a feeling swelled in me. I thought of the collective effort made by parents and friends and grandparents and aunts and uncles and teachers and therapists and who knew who else that had been required for each individual there to know their gender, assert it, and then get themselves to New England.

As your mom, I've tried to become aware of everything I don't know about being trans. I don't know what it's like to experience gender dysphoria. I don't know what it's like to date or search for a mate when people make the wrong assumptions about your body. I have no idea what it's like to create your own aligned puberty with a shot of testosterone once a week. I have no idea what it will be like to go to college on "T" or what it will be like to travel with syringes. Everything I know about trans sex came from the copy of *Confessions of the Fox* by Jordy Rosenberg, that novel I'd snuck onto your night table. I read it with the same ferocity that

I read *Forever* by Judy Blume when I was 13, although I felt more embarrassed about it, like maybe I was spying on something that I should not have been, even as I also felt relieved, like I had at least found something, some material, to help me talk with you the same way I've talked with your sisters. You need friends and mentors, people your age, and folks a little farther along the road to talk about the intimacies of your life that I can never really understand. As we arrived at camp, I hoped you would find that community at camp.

When the counselor doing the lice check finished running his fingers along your scalp, he said, "Dude, you have amazing hair." I saw you blush. He had seen you and knew how to read you. I wondered if it was fun for you to be seen not just as a boy this time, but also as a trans boy with good-looking hair. Then he gave you a nod to let you know you were good to go and pointed to the door where we picked up your cabin assignment.

Your cabin was like every other camp cabin I had ever seen, a simple wooden structure with screen windows and bunk beds lining the perimeter of the room. A couple of boys your age milled around trying to pick a bunk. Two counselors came up and introduced themselves. Jennifer told us they used they/them pronouns, and Clay, the other counselor, said they used the same. You picked a top bunk. And after you marked your chosen bunk with your backpack, we went outside and sat on a picnic table under a clutch of pine trees.

Across the lawn I heard girls giggling in another cabin. I followed the sound of their chirping voices and strained to make out their figures through a screened window across the way. I saw a sleeping bag with pastel peace signs along with a string of twinkly lights pinned in the crease of the roof line. Girls were hugging each other and making animated gestures with their hands. You hunkered in next to me, quiet. You wanted to wait for the absolute last minute to say good-bye. Looking down at the grains of wood in the table, you took a couple of deep breaths and pressed the heels of your hands into your eyes. Then you tugged at the bottom seam of your t-shirt to wipe away some tears. My insides felt like overripe fruit, soft and weepy, but I put on a brave face. "Saying goodbye is sometimes like facing a cold swimming pool. Better to just jump in fast and get moving," I said. Then I squeezed my arm around your shoulders, pantomiming positivity. Maybe my forced good cheer would cast a spell of courage on you.

We walked back to the cabin to find your counselor. I pointed out that one of your bunkmates had also just settled in. "I bet you'll be friends by dinner," I whispered into your ear. But you were barely listening to me. Your eyes scanned the room. Your hands were in your pockets. I could see that you had put on a brave face, too, and had already covered up your feelings from the picnic table. I wanted to look right into your eyes and say something wise, but I started to tear up. I turned my face, looked over your shoulder and gave you the best hug I could. I told you I loved you, and then I beat a path for the cabin's screen door.

On my way out, I spotted your giant duffle bag on top of a mountain of other bags sitting beside your cabin door. It looked in place, stacked with its mates. I remembered how critical fitting in had been to me at your age and imagined that you felt the same. I worried that being a trans kid without a coming out story, without the same kind of struggle many of your fellow campers had likely had, you might feel chronically between worlds, not the same as your cis peers at home, but also not the same as your trans peers at camp. How heavy it would feel to always be hauling a full pack between communities, never really able to unload. I wished, then, that we had talked about how much of my own life had been wasted trying to fit in, how I felt too progressive among my schoolmates and suburban peers, and too conventional among my feminist and writer colleagues. Belonging only came to me when I realized that the most sustaining connection came through the love I felt from a small handful of people—from Dad, from Nonny, from you and your sisters, and from a couple of friends. What I received from them wasn't so much acceptance as permission to belong to myself, to be in a state of continuous discovery about the shape of my relationship to the world around me. I wished I had told you that finding comfort in my own skin and my own story turned out to be more important than fitting in ever was.

Walking back to the car, I stopped and sat for a minute by the waterfront. I saw the bath house, the dock that extended out into the lake, the huge blue and green float on the water. I remembered my own camp, the temporary refuge it had been for me during my childhood summers. It never solved the problem of feeling between worlds, but those few weeks of canoeing and crafts and evening singing by a campfire always felt like a warm-hearted respite. For a few weeks every year, I felt like I could take a break from my usual social worries. The days were easy. They started and ended with singing. The friendships, free of the push and pull of a whole school year's worth of social dynamics, were clear and genuine and lasting. I took a seat on a stump by the lakefront and said a little prayer to the water and the trees and the chipmunks I saw scrambling over a pile of logs. I imagined you running in a game of tag, swimming out along the pier, eating in the hot dining hall. Laughing with your new summer friends.

When I returned to pick you up, my heart pounded. Parents in cars repeated the assembly line procedures from drop-off day. Our caravan inched along the bumpy unmarked road that traced the edge of the lake. I rolled my windows down and let the New England summer air fill the interior of the rental I had picked up in Boston. I checked in with the counselor at the security checkpoint. Then I parked by the side of the road and joined all the other parents who lined up outside the dining hall. In the doorway, someone with a clipboard checked your name off a list.

The dining hall was as crowded as an airport at Thanksgiving, and just as busy. I saw pairs of parents hugging their campers, counselors pointing this way and that way, a table with piles of camp sweatshirts for sale, and a few counselors managing the cash box. It was hard to find you in the swarm of bodies and activity. Eventually I spied you all the way on the other side of the room. Before waving wildly, I took a minute to watch you. You were sitting on a picnic bench laughing with two other boys. The sun on your hair looked electric. You threw your hand in front of you like you were punching the air, and the boys around tucked into themselves as they laughed. Just then, you turned your head and caught my eye. I waved like a maniac—do you remember? I jangled my arms all around. I brought both my hands to my mouth and blew you kisses. You rolled your eyes and waved me over, but the line was long, and I had to be patient, which felt impossible. When I finally made my way through the crowd, you put your arms around me and gave me a kiss on the cheek. "Mom! Meet my friends." We chatted for a little bit, then went outside and hauled your huge bag off the top of the mountain of duffle bags.

Driving away from camp, I felt like a Labrador retriever waiting to fetch my favorite chew toy. I was nearly panting, wanting to hear every detail about how camp went. But every mother of a teenager knows there is no faster way to shut down a conversation with their kid than to appear eager. So, with considerable restraint, in hopes of evoking some choice bit of information from you, I played at being nonchalant. I limited myself to one laid-back question: "So, how was it?"

You told me it was okay. Really? Just okay? That was all I was going to get? It had looked so much more promising than that at pick-up. You stared at the window silently for a few more minutes.

We had a three-hour car ride ahead, and I held on to hope that you'd let your guard down. It took about half an hour before you told me about the boys who had arrived at camp the week before you, and how it had taken a day or two for you to break into the group. You told me that Riley, whom we had met that first day, did end up being a friend after all. Then you described tubing and climbing and campfires. The terrible food. The grimy shower stalls that you had to clean. You told me that the real talking happened at night while you all lay in your bunks. Friends talked about testosterone—the shots and the patches. You learned that some trans guys opt to go through some of their puberty to harvest their eggs. You found out that your counselor Clay was going to medical school and that he had been an EMT (emergency medical technician) before that, something that you have always wanted to be. You met your camp director, who is a trans man with a degree in social work. You were a blizzard of stories.

Then your phone started pinging. You typed with fury, your face bunching and stretching, flickering as if the conversation were happening right there, in our car. It was a group chat. You told me. With your camp friends. You planned to keep in touch all year.

REFLECTION QUESTIONS

- How do you create sanctuary for your child? What is your own experience of sanctuary? Where do you feel safest? Where do you travel in your mind when you want to calm yourself down? What do you know about where your child experiences feelings of safety and belonging?
- Is there a trans community you and your child have joined or might join? Is there a place that your family has designated as a location where you can promise your child their gender will always be honored, no questions asked? What do you think sanctuary for your child's gender would require?
- What would a conversation about sanctuary look like between you and your child? How could it be a soothing conversation for both of you? How could you draw on imagination and storytelling?

Letter 10
July 2019: Developmental Disruptions

Walking into Diane Ehrensaft's office with Dad, I felt an unexpected sense of relief. I had read her books years before arriving in her office. They are near biblical for parents of gender-expansive kids, so when I learned that she kept her office in the Bay Area, I thought it was worth trying to see her. I didn't expect to get in with someone I thought of as famous, but she got back to me so quickly that I scolded myself for not trying to call her sooner.

Her office reminded me of Nonny's where she saw her clients in her Jungian therapy practice. There was a tray for sand play, which Nonny did not have, but, like Nonny's office, her small space was full of figurines. She had puppets of pirates and alligators and tiny statues of soldiers and babies and cats and dogs. Some of her figures wore dark, frightening faces and others projected friendly smiles. All of them appeared frozen in their ongoing drama. I could almost see the many tiny hands of her young patients bringing the figures to life as they worked through their own stories and questions.

The figurines that felt the most familiar to me were three stone bears set on a small table near Diane's chair. Their backs curved gently like eggs, and miniature medicine bundles appeared strapped onto their midline. When I was a teenager, Nonny and I had traveled together to New Mexico, and on that trip she had selected two similar bear figurines, which she also kept in her office. In many indigenous American tribes, bears symbolize the spirit of the western direction. They are thought to conjure healing, incubation, and powerful mothering instincts. I had often imagined the scenes that Nonny's bears had witnessed, and how in their own way the borrowed symbols had accrued a gravitas that stood for Nonny's time spent caring for others. Whether Diane's bears had accompanied her in her therapy practice as long as Nonny's had, I couldn't know. But I experienced them with a familiar reverence that gave me comfort.

On the way to the appointment, I had asked Dad to tell our family story. I had told it so many times to so many professionals that it had lost some of the freshness that comes with an early telling. My narrative had acquired a life of its own that had to do with the way I remembered it. I wanted to hear Dad's version, to find out the details that stood out to him, and to understand the sequences that had made the biggest impression on his thinking.

He described the first time you cut your hair, how we used "-ish" to soften the association between things that were traditionally "for boys" and things that were traditionally "for girls," by describing them as "boyish" or "girlish." Dad also remembered the jogger with the black shorts that you told me you wanted to look like. And he mentioned the nervous jokes that started to come up more and more often as your older sister developed—the way you sometimes jumped around in your room pretending you had "coconuts." I had written your jokes in the notes I kept but had forgotten about them. It was a detail that reminded me about the anxiety you felt about growing into a woman's body.

After listening to Dad, Diane said that she heard clues about your gender identity and encouraged us to continue bringing your gender into focus the way we had been doing. She assured us that we were in great hands with Korina Zee, your endocrinologist, and apologized for how our first appointment at the clinic had rattled us. I didn't realize she was a part of that team. She asked if she could pass on our feedback about our experience, and we agreed.

Then we shifted the focus of our conversation to your fertility. Instead of focusing specifically on fertility, she encouraged us to broaden our frame of reference by considering family-building holistically. She offered her observation that gender identity was an important foundation for most people, and especially for people with gender dysphoria, it had a primacy that usually superseded other developmental milestones. Dad put his hand on my back. And with his touch I started to tremble. This was the conclusion I had already come to during my visit with Dr. Henderson, but visiting the topic again, I felt split open by grief.

"I think I sense an open wound," Diane said. Her voice was soft like cashmere, warm and comfortable. It signaled to me that it was alright for this dilemma to be difficult; we could love and support you and still feel broken by the complexity of the journey. She explained that for you and for us, the need to consider your fertility at this age and stage was a developmental disruption—an event that interrupted and destabilized the more typical timeline that young adolescents and their parents follow. When she explained it this way, it seemed obvious that the premature timing of these considerations forced all three of us, you, me and Dad, to take responsibility for an aspect of your life that should be on hold for at least another decade. Her explanation didn't make the pain of making grave decisions for your future-self go away, but it relieved me of the loneliness I felt in grieving the process of our decision-making. Noticing that my concerns showed up in my psyche as a kind of wound felt accurate.

I never grieved your identity, but I often grieved the context in which you've had to live it. I've grieved the lack of education in the adults around us, the loss of the progress that gender-diverse people gained during the Obama administration, and that the cutting-edge technology to support you was only in its first decade. And I grieved my own grief, the way it crowded daily life in our family, the way it darkened my vision of your future with disappointment about your fertility and fears about the challenges you might face because of your gender.

There was a way of looking at the world around us in which it seemed like you were living through one of the best times to be alive as a gender-diverse person. Two years prior, *Time* magazine claimed we had reached the transgender "tipping point." You'd been to a camp for trans kids, for goodness' sakes. But while the increase in trans visibility seemed to increase acceptance in part of the population, it also seemed to increase intolerance in equal or greater measure in another part of the population. And visibility alone would not improve technology or make it safer for you to live in the many states that did not offer protection against discrimination for the trans community. I knew other people had faced much worse than you did, and still I grieved.

As we left Diane's office, she asked if I was planning to attend this year's Gender Spectrum conference, where she would be speaking. When I told her I was, she suggested I attend her session on family building. I made a mental note to be there. Dad and I thanked her for her time with us, and then we left. Back on the street, we headed toward a casual restaurant I had been to once and thought Dad would like. It was late in the day. The concrete of the sidewalk, the rippled surface of Lake Merritt, and the pale building facades all sparkled in the sharp afternoon sun.

"I can't believe I missed the boat on the fertility thing," I said. It still came as a shock to me that all those years when we thought of you as middle gender, when I had in the back of my mind that maybe, someday, we would find out about blockers, I never once considered your fertility. Dad and I walked along silently for a bit before a thought of your sisters struck me. "Well, our family is not short on eggs at least," I said, only half joking. Dad laughed back and made note that their genetic material was practically the same as yours. "It could totally work," he said, as if we had finally found a solution. I clucked and shook my head thinking about how absurd it would be to disrupt all of your lives that way, as if multiple disruptions could mend our broken timeline the way multiplying negatives could make a positive.

I was beginning to accept that we were going to let go of your future fertility. It felt like loosening my grip in a tug of war. I wanted you to have fertility options—I did. I thought that you and your gender-diverse peers deserved to be cared for by adults who were working hard to make more options possible. And I felt less panicked, less like the trajectory of your future came down to me personally. If there were options, I thought we had started to meet the people who could help us access them. I could research and question and call as many doctors as possible, and I still could not change the decade in which you were born. My jaw and back and belly relaxed. Dad put his hand on my shoulder, and I leaned into his chest.

When we were still living in our old house, there was a night when we were all sitting around our wooden table in the kitchen for dinner and you asked, "What age do you want to live to?"

Nonny was there, and she said she wanted to live to be 96. Alison claimed 77, which sounded impossibly old to her. I passed on answering the question; it gave me a funny superstitious feeling, like if I said a number, I would change my whole future. Then we all looked at Dad. He turned his head squarely toward mine, a thin skim of tears rose in the brims of his eyes. I knew what he was going to say.

"Three hundred."

"You think we'll make it?" I asked. He was talking about actuarial escape velocity, an idea popularized by Ray Kurzweil, one of his colleagues at Google, who had posited that in the next one hundred years, humanity would out-engineer death.

"I think we could," he sighed. "But if we don't, we'll be right behind the wave."

I felt that way after the meeting with Diane. You were part of a cohort of gender-expansive kids who were living through both the good fortune and risks associated with V. 1.0 of any technical advancement. Dad and I had lived and worked in the Valley long enough to know the highs and lows of V 1.0. So many of the lows came from perceiving the horizon, but not quite making it there.

REFLECTION QUESTIONS

- Parenting any child is both joyful and complicated. As a parent, situations in which we have less control than we would like bring up a lot of feelings. What aspects of your child's journey feel complicated to you? Where do you experience the loss of control? What fears does it bring up for you?

- How are you proud of your child's identity? When do you experience the intuitive "knowing" that you have your child's identity in focus? What personal values and traits have you brought to the process of supporting your child? What would it be like to anchor yourself in those values and traits and know you are doing the best you can, the best that any parent can when stewarding children toward their own adult lives?

Letter 11

July 2019: Gender Spectrum

One single image. A new mother with dark hair sitting in a hospital bed holding her baby. It was maybe the tenth slide in Diane Ehrensaft's family-building lecture at Gender Spectrum. The young woman had survived childhood cancer. During her treatment, her mother had insisted on removing and preserving one of her ovaries before the start of her treatment. The baby in the photograph had been conceived after the woman's own ovary had been thawed and stitched back into her body. The new mother was not trans, but this single image was evidence that the technology to preserve your fertility was at least in development. I didn't know why Diane had not mentioned this in our meeting; maybe these ideas are still so experimental that she did not want to give me hope. I think she sensed that I had grief bottled up inside, and she knew that processing it was important, regardless of how the technology developed.

The long drive to Gender Spectrum would have been worth it if all I came home with was that one image. But there was so much more than that. For two days, a community of clinicians, professionals, and families with gender-expansive children took over a small college campus. Moms, dads, and grandparents mingled with doctors, psychologists, teachers, and thought leaders to collaborate on how to provide better care and support for gender-expansive kids. The Transgender Law Center took over an office, where they assisted with paperwork to update identification records. At night there was a big party with games and clothing exchanges, and the best, a station for haircuts. It was the longest running conference in the country that addressed caring for gender-expansive youth. I wished I had started coming sooner, but during the years when I felt skeptical about the gender dysphoria diagnosis, I worried the conference would be too focused on pathology for me to feel comfortable. I had been wrong.

Diane Ehrensaft had been involved in the organization for many years, and the annual conference was imbued with her caring, open-minded approach. Even in the workshop that was potentially one of the most controversial—a session for therapists to brainstorm approaches to working with unsupportive parents—the leaders focused on helping families stay connected while they navigated their children's gender explorations. The session worked through case studies in which parents did not support their children's gender identity, giving therapists and doctors and physicians' assistants the opportunity to grapple with the fact that trans children usually fared better mentally, physically, and emotionally, when they were able to stay in contact with their parents even when the parents needed a lot of education. So, rather than treating parents as gatekeepers to work around, the group collaborated on ways to keep parents engaged and learning during what was often a difficult adjustment.

The data is clear here. When families support their trans children, their children's mental health outcomes are significantly better. But I don't underestimate how difficult it would be to encourage adults to revise their views on gender. In some families, if parents support their children, they will also lose support from their communities and even other family members. It was clear in the meeting that the professionals felt torn up about how to support kids who were not in supportive families. On the one hand, they knew they were possibly the only adult in the child's world who believed what was happening to them. On the other hand, it was clear to the professionals that these parents were doing emotional harm to their children when they refused to support them. Still, keeping difficult parents engaged was one of the most important actions to take on the children's behalf. This is challenging therapeutic work and is not always successful. It explains why so much of our local youth homeless population is part of the LGBTQ+ community—sometimes it is easier just to leave than to keep trying to stay.

Later in the conference I attended a session with Dr. Aida Kim, a reproductive endocrinologist from the University of California at San Francisco. Petite, stylish, and upbeat, her good cheer contrasted with how serious her cutting-edge research was. She presented a series of studies that considered the impact of cross-sex hormones on the fertility of trans adults. Hormone therapy for adults who transitioned after puberty had reduced fertility, but in the case of trans men, pregnancy was still possible. The research didn't apply to you, because you would not be experiencing an estrogen puberty, whereas the trans men in the study had completed puberty before starting testosterone. Her research signaled to me that she was one of the innovators who had her sights on the horizon for you. At the end of her presentation, she asked a penetrating question. She wanted to know why more trans kids weren't coming in to talk to her.

Since our first visit to the gender clinic, the Endocrine Society had updated their clinical guidelines to encourage physicians to discuss fertility preservation with the gender-diverse kids they treated. And still, patients and their families were not scheduling consults with her. The audience, which appeared to be mostly doctors, did not have much of a reply for her. I raised my hand and took a chance explaining how the developmental disruption of thinking about your fertility had felt in our own family. At first you didn't want to discuss it and insisted that adoption was fine for you (and it still might be!). But after you had been on blockers for a while and were no longer preoccupied about how you were going to grow up, you seemed to have more mental space to think about your long-term future.

On one of the last mornings of your seventh-grade year, you and I stood near the sink in the kitchen. Dad sat between Alison and Lizzie at the counter and started to scroll through his "This year in history" app, a little program he hacked together for us—our own custom-made digital record of family life. First, he read out phrases that Lizzie had said on that same date in May way back when she was two. Then he started flipping through photographs. You and your sisters at the end of the school year, standing in front of the school sign. You with your fourth-grade teacher. And then one of you and Alison and Lizzie with Mrs. Bryant—the one teacher in all of your school years that the three of you had all had.

Right then you tapped me on the shoulder and made a come closer gesture with your hand. You wanted to tell me something private and needed me to lean my ear close to you. "I think I want to have my own baby," you whispered. You were 13. I knew then that you understood the stakes of the path you were on, and that you were processing more about your adult future than you were able to when you were not able to envision growing up. In the conference room, I shared the thought that it could be possible that many families—in addition to not having the resources or options necessary to ask questions about their trans children's fertility—possibly struggled as they emerged from the first developmental hurdle of settling the matter of gender identity. By the time they did, even if they had the resources, perhaps the family system was too exhausted, too worn out by conflict to consider yet another fraught issue. Or maybe they were just afraid. Afraid of experimental treatments. Afraid of attracting additional attention to their child. There were limitless obstacles to addressing a trans child's future fertility.

We addressed your fertility, at least in part, because of my young adulthood. There was a perfect overlap between what I had studied and my old wounds around having to fend for myself. That your fertility did not seem as important a consideration in the transition guidelines as I thought it should offended my feminist sensibilities and woke up dormant anger I had about not getting what I needed as a young woman. Fending for myself at that age had made me alert to next steps and especially committed to advocating for you and your sisters. I hated being unprepared, and my energy to fight for you three was almost indefatigable, which was not always a good thing. I had a tendency to overprotect, and I counted on Dad to balance me out. But in his mind, your fertility came down to a technical problem, an area where he was likely to be as obsessive as I was. If the science was out there, he wanted you to have it. After our meeting with Diane, I had started to accept that we were facing a problem we might not be able to solve—that we needed to resign to whatever the future held. But at the slightest hint of possibility, we were both back at it.

After Dr. Kim's presentation, I introduced myself to her. Up close she was even more petite than she had seemed during her presentation. She smiled, and behind her large round glasses, her eyebrows rose in friendly arcs. I told her about you and about the questions we had about preserving your fertility. She invited me to make an appointment for you at her clinic and gave me her cell phone number to contact her directly if we had any problems making an appointment.

As soon as I got home, I called her office to schedule a time with her, and began to research oophorectomies, the surgical removal of the ovaries. The procedure that had made my insides quiver in Dr. Zee's office a year ago now had more context—a photograph of a woman with her baby, a physician whom I could imagine trusting with a procedure like this. It had normalized just enough for me to begin to see it as a possibility. In the course of my rooting around, I learned that the pediatric oncology community had been exploring fertility preservation options for years for children whose fertility was endangered by their cancer treatments for years. I found a paper from 2013 (four years before we first showed up at the gender clinic) that suggested physicians share fertility preservation options with parents before their children started treatments.

Knowing that a group of scientists had been actively pursuing solutions to pediatric iatrogenic infertility (that is, childhood infertility caused by a medically necessary treatment) was exciting, it was a strand of hope. But realizing the research had been going on for four years before our first appointment at the gender clinic rekindled my sense of injustice. Was one group of children's fertility more important, more worth saving, than another's? The thought stabbed at me like a hot fire poker. A friend of mine who knew more about infertility treatments than I did told me not to take this discovery so personally, because the whole field of infertility treatment was pocked with issues of inequity. She was probably right, but it didn't change how I felt, which was angry. Rather than let it burn through me, I was determined to channel my energy into generating possibilities.

REFLECTION QUESTIONS

- What are the obstacles your child faces in day-to-day life? What would it be like to make a list of these topics and to prioritize them? How could it support your mental health and your child's mental health to have your worries written down on paper and to commit to handling problems one at a time (rather than ruminating about the list of topics in your mind)?
- How much does anxiety influence your day-to-day? Your child's day-to-day? What strategies do you use to manage anxiety? What style of coping is common in your family? What would it be like to keep a visible list of coping strategies and tools someplace where your child could see and remember these ideas in hard times?
- Growing up trans and raising a trans child can feel very, very stressful. How can you normalize some of the stress that your child experiences? What aspects of friendship dynamics, for example, are common to all kids? What

> would it be like to be in conversation with your child about the difference between the common stressors of childhood and the particular minority stress of growing up trans? How might this differentiation impact the coping strategies that you and your family engage?

Interview

Kelley Blair on Alternate Perspectives to Western Medicine in Transgender Care

Kelley B. Blair MS, LPC, is a licensed professional counselor with nearly 20 years of experience working in the helping field with therapeutic and advocacy experience related directly to the LGBTQ and Native American communities in Oklahoma. Kelley is Choctaw, Cherokee, and Seminole, also identifying as bisexual as well as Two-Spirit. Kelley is the founder of the Diversity Center of Oklahoma,* a non-profit outpatient mental health treatment agency providing services to the gender-diverse population and their families, including disenfranchised and marginalized people of color.

In 2014, Kelley organized an annual LGBTQ mental health symposium in Oklahoma to increase mental health professionals' continuing education and cultural competency training for the gender-diverse community. Kelley currently co-chairs the Central Oklahoma Two Spirit Society and sits on the International Council of Two Spirit Societies. Kelley has earned a Master's in Community Counseling as well as a Bachelor's in Behavioral

* www.diversitycenterofoklahoma.org

Science. Kelley is dedicated to making communities inclusive for gender-diverse persons and for persons of color.

Cristina: Kelley, you identify as Two-Spirit. How did you come to know you were Two-Spirit, and what does that term mean to you?

Kelley: I've always felt like I was a masculine female. Growing up I saw myself as a tomboy. Even as an adult, people would make comments like, "You clean up nice," when I would wear make-up and look more feminine. I never heard the term "Two-Spirit" until I was about 40, and when I understood the meaning, I knew that described me. But even at the time I didn't share it with many people. That, too, is a coming out process, which meant I had to accept and share with others that I was not congruent with the body I was born into, and that feeling is culturally specific. As a Native person and feeling very connected to my spiritual self, the concept of being Two-Spirit made sense to me. I finally felt congruent in my body as who I am. But I don't feel congruent in the cultural constructs that exist in White culture. For me, my gender and sexual orientation is a spiritual blending. My attraction to both men and women regardless of whether they are cisgender or gender-diverse is natural and dates back to pre-colonial days. I tell people I am Two-Spirit, transgender/gender nonconforming. When I do trainings, I tell my audience I am Two-Spirit, Choctaw, Cherokee, and Seminole, and as a Native person I feel very congruent in my body, but the western side of me does not feel congruent. I consider myself transgender because my experience matches how western culture describes the transgender experience. In both of my cultures I don't fit into gender norms, so I tell folx I am gender nonconforming.

Two-Spirit is an umbrella term used to reflect and restore Indigenous traditions that were forcefully suppressed by means of colonization and historical trauma, honoring the fluid, diverse nature of gender, attraction, and its connection to a sense of community and spirituality. The term Two-Spirit is used by some Indigenous people rather than, or in addition to, identifying as 2S-LGBTQ+. The term Two-Spirit is translated from the Northern Algonquin word, *niizh manitoag*, and is used by some American Indian/First Nation people and communities to signify gender and sexual orientation variance. Two-Spirit is said to come from a dream from an elder named Myra Laramee. The term Two-Spirit is an addition, not a replacement, for Indigenous languages that already have a word for gender and sexual orientation variance.

Cristina: When I visited you in Oklahoma City you talked to me about the medicine wheel. Can you describe how you think of the medicine wheel and the way you use it to counsel gender-diverse folx who visit the Diversity Center? How does this approach both differ and/or support the western model of medical transition?

Kelley: As a young therapist, I worked as a vocational rehabilitation therapist for a tribe. I was supervised by a clinical psychologist and my immediate supervisor was a Master's level therapist. When I first started working there, I remember telling my supervisor that I kept visualizing something in my head when I was working with clients. The object was round, like a circle, though not like a shield. She kept telling me I would understand its significance when the time was right. A few months later we went to a national conference for vocational therapists in Seattle, Washington. There were a couple hundred people there. I remember listening to a Native medical doctor who talked about the importance of helping our people and helping them find balance in their lives. As counselors it was important to address all aspects of the person, their physical, mental, spiritual, community, and emotional needs. He put a picture of the medicine wheel up on the screen. I looked over my shoulder and somewhat loudly told my boss "That's what I've been seeing!" Those around me began to smile and giggle. I guess they understood this part Native person coming into their balance. Understanding the medicine wheel changed how I viewed so many things in my life, and it changed how I worked with folx.

When I started the Diversity Center of Oklahoma, it was set up with the medicine wheel structure in mind. If we weren't addressing all of aspects of balance in our treatment—physical, mental, spiritual, community, and emotional aspects—we weren't assisting the whole person. If we couldn't provide those services directly at first, we tried to provide linkage to those services until we could provide them directly.

Cristina: You live in a state that is actively working toward (or might have already passed) legislation that would restrict access to gender-affirming care. How is that impacting you and your community in the day-to-day? How is the community responding to take care of one another and to fight for access to care?

Kelley: This is a very challenging question. Many aspects of care are still up in the air for us. We have families that are very concerned about how they will be able to provide hormone treatment and counseling for their children. We aren't sure how the laws will affect us in providing services to adults. We are always worried about our funding, especially for our transgender folx. If we lose the funding, we will have to close our physical doors. We may also have to look into providing services online. We have folx exploring the development of some kind of underground railroad system to move families to safety. The hate is increasing, and we have to keep our doors locked here at the center.

Letter 12
August 2019: Truth Bomb

All summer I let myself believe the issues at school had resolved. The school had put a lot of energy into communicating their inclusivity policy to parents, to teachers, and in the classroom. You seemed happy and comfortable, but one day the phone rang and a good mom friend of mine said, "I have something I need you to know." I felt my stomach drop. Her son had been in tennis lessons with another boy in your class, Cooper, and while there he overheard a conversation in which Cooper had learned your birth name.

It wasn't clear to me what Cooper knowing your gender history would mean for you. But I was nervous. So, like a bad game of telephone, I hung up from the call and immediately dialed Cooper's mom. She had been a great friend to me, and an honest advocate for you, so I hoped together we could prevent further harm. She promised she'd sit down with Cooper and explain that what he had learned was private information that should not have been shared and should not be passed on. I wanted to believe that Cooper would have your back, but I just did not know.

The threat that anyone at your new school could learn your history and share it had always lurked in the background of our decision to change schools. Last spring, I worried constantly that you would be outed. But when we finally made it to summer, I assumed everything would be okay.

I was with your older sister when I received this most recent news, and she was even more alarmed than I was. She pointed to my phone and said I had to call you right away after talking to Cooper's mom. From her own middle school years, she felt a rising sense of terror for you. The urgent look in her eyes revealed how easy it was for her to imagine your private information running rampant on Snapchat or Instagram or Discord. It was such a relief after I called you that your social media accounts did not show anything out of the ordinary. It appeared that Cooper's mom had managed to pull it off. I don't know how she talked to Cooper, but he proved himself to be a good citizen. Still, knowing that he had your personal information felt like watching the fuse burn on a stick of dynamite. Is this how it felt for you too? Did you fall asleep at night wondering about what kind of information someone might drop into the internet?

When you walked through the kitchen door later that day, the thought popped into my head that summer looked good on you. You had grown a bit taller, the scattering of new freckles across your nose gave you an outdoorsy look, and your shoulders had broadened just a bit so that t-shirts pulled smoothly across your chest and back. I got the feeling you didn't want to discuss what had happened, but after failing to calculate how high the social stakes were about your gender once before, I felt desperate to get ahead of this potential catastrophe.

So that night I sat next to you on the couch and told you I thought we should have a plan in place in case things went poorly. I asked you if you wanted to be stealth, to keep your history a secret for as long as possible, but you didn't. That has never been your plan. You didn't want secrecy; you wanted control—to tell your story in your own words at a time that felt right to you. When you reflected on what it might be like for you at school if someone did end up sharing your gender history, you felt the other students would support you. I asked if there was anyone in particular you thought could stand by you if that happened. You named your friend Rowan. "Maybe you should tell him before school starts," I suggested, "just so you have someone to go to if things get rough." You thought about it, and then suggested we have him over for a visit. "I guess I am going to have a coming out story after all," you said.

I sense you are going to have a lot of coming out stories. You are so easily read as a boy that the longer you live a boy's life, the less likely it will be that people you meet will make the correct assumption about your history.

I asked if you wanted to talk to Rowan at the beginning of your visit, just to get it over with. You shook your head. "After I drop that truth bomb? No way." I was stunned again by my cluelessness. Who knew how Rowan was going to take it? You suggested we go get frozen yogurt right before he went home so that you could tell him without worrying too much about what would happen next. But of course, once we got to the froyo place, Rowan ran into three kids he knew. We chatted with his friends for what felt like an interminable amount of time, eating froyo, your knee bouncing under the table. I watched you watch Rowan and felt like you two lived on different planets right then. He inhabited space with his friends with no knowledge at all of what was going on for you. Your nervousness created an atmosphere all its own. When we climbed back in the car your separate atmospheres converged.

I held tight to the steering wheel and my heart batted inside my ribs. I heard you say, "Hey, Rowan. I have something to tell you." He laughed and made a silly remark that I can't remember. You two usually joked around a lot, and he wasn't ready for what was coming. Later, when I looked at the essay you wrote about this moment, your description blew me away: *My heart was racing faster than the car, and I could feel my words in my throat. "I..." I stuttered. And then it came out. Each syllable...like lava, oozing and unstoppable. "I'm trans."* In the car I held my breath and clenched my whole body. I forced myself to keep my eyes on the road. Then Rowan said one simple line, "That doesn't change anything." A tide of tears flooded my eyes. When you told him the story of what had been happening, he cringed. He knew how some of the boys in the year could be. Then he promised to "yeeto" them if anyone caused you any trouble.

Rowan's perception of you seemed unshaken by this new information. I had hoped this would be true. Abstract information about your history was a weak force in comparison to all the first-hand experiences Rowan had had with you.

I started to think about the first time you performed on stage as Jake for your new middle school community. You were the lead singer in one of the rock band performances. Your song: "Scar Tissue" by the Red Hot Chili Peppers. At first your back was toward the audience. You had on your white blazer and pants, an outfit that had inexplicable star quality. When the music started, you turned around. You closed your eyes and grabbed the mic as you sang. We could see the beat move through you as you gestured to the crowd with your free hand. You carried the sad triumph of the tune as if it belonged to you.

My phone started to vibrate as some of my mom friends texted me with messages. "OMG, your son," and, "Jake is amazing." I looked at the sea of heads in the crowd, watching them all watch you and your swagger coming alive right before our eyes. You, the boy named Jake, reflected in every pair of nearly a thousand eyes. This was what we had been working toward. This was why we had moved. I felt your true self searing into the shared mind of an entire community.

In the car ride with Rowan, I understood that the impact of the concert, and all the smaller moments that followed, added up to something permanent. Once you were held in the minds of others as a boy, once the relationship between you was built on the shared assumption of your masculinity, that experience felt so powerfully true and congruent that for Rowan—and I imagined for many people you've known at your new school—any information about your gender assigned at birth had been robbed of some of its potency. The strange thing wasn't that you felt like a boy inside, but that anyone ever made the mistake of thinking you were a girl.

Letter 13

September 2019: Coming to Your Senses

I loved watching you laugh when we were out to dinner with Nonny last night. I had never seen you observe your young self the way you did when you were watching those old videos on her phone. There you were on her little screen, seven and eight years old, a jumble of disorganized motion, a swirl of kid chaos. In one of the videos, I am sitting at the dining room table with Lizzie snuggled into my lap. I am whispering something in her ear. And then you fly into the frame like a missile. You're dressed as Luke Skywalker, and you zip behind our chair and out of the other side of the frame, only to come back a second later, flinging your head around and flapping your arms so hard that your white costume top slips halfway off.

When you watched the video, you started cracking up. I leaned over to look at it, and then I started laughing too. Soon enough the laughter from our table was filling the whole restaurant. Other people eating turned and stared. In the middle of your laughing, you called yourself "kid amplified" and asked how I dealt with you. I told you that you were interesting, unique, original. "What a crock," you said through your breathless guffaws. You suspected, like you often do, that I was sugar-coating things.

The truth is, when you were that age, something observable was going on—which was why I went to see all of those psychologists. And even though I rejected the idea that you had gender dysphoria back then, I still thought you needed support. You were uncomfortable. It looked like something was tumbling in your body to me. Sometimes you waved your limbs with excess energy, flapping them around like rubber bands snapping. You acted impulsively and craved physical impact. You wanted to wrestle and play tackle football and jump from heights. When you were little and we sat at the dinner table, you tapped out rhythms with your fork and knife constantly. At school, teachers gave you squeeze balls or putty to keep your hands busy. You were never still. There was a restlessness in you that seemed to emanate from the inside out.

And sometimes you had tantrums. They were so explosive, we had to give them their own name: slamwhams. In those moments, you shook with frustration. You screamed. You threw things. A few times you kicked Alison in the shin. None of this seemed like it would be helped by a lot of sitting and talking. So instead of continuing to meet with psychologists, I took you to an occupational therapist who was known in my mom network for supporting children who had trouble self-regulating.

Leslie had an office with steel loops in the ceiling from which she hung hammocks and swings. There were gymnastic mats on the floor, and foam blocks the size of small couches stacked up along the walls. Unlike the psychologists, who often postulated about your gender even before meeting you, Leslie had nothing to say until she laid her own eyes on you. In that first appointment, she started by offering you a swing in the middle of the room and letting you rock back and forth as hard as you wanted. You pumped the pendulum of the swing to its maximum arc with enough effort that you got short of breath. When you were done with that, you climbed the foam blocks to a perch up by the ceiling. When you were ready you jumped the six or eight feet down to the mat on the floor. After that, you shot yourself like a cannonball across the room into foam pads that were leaned up on the far wall.

What I noticed that day was that my own body winced in the presence of this kind of rough play. My skin gripped and my shoulders tensed in anticipation of getting whacked by your flying body, even though I knew we weren't likely to collide. The breeze that rushed by my face as you pumped Leslie's swing or launched yourself across the room was enough to trigger my own sensory response. The impact and motion you sought led my body to involuntarily retreat. You were a Border Collie puppy born to parents who were life-long library cats. At the very least, that first appointment with Leslie taught me that you needed other adults in your life to help you move and play the way that felt most natural to you.

Over the course of your work with Leslie, she introduced us to a kid-friendly program for self-regulation called The Alert Program®.* The idea behind it was that every family member had a sensory engine with high and low points during the day, and with the right kinds of conversations, we could plan for what each of us needed. We used this new language to talk about the energy in your body and the way you craved being in motion so much of the time. In private, Leslie told me that she thought you might have mild sensory processing disorder, a condition in which sensory information can overload a child's neuro-processing function and cause a "traffic jam" in the brain and body.

* www.alertprogram.com

Kids with this condition often needed extra sensory inputs. She thought that the intense play you did in her office could be evidence of this kind of sensory need. Swinging generated increased vestibular input (which is also what you gave yourself when you swung your head around wildly at home or at school), and roughhousing, with all its blunt impact on your body and compaction of your joints, was a way that you were creating proprioceptive input for yourself. I had never heard of the vestibular system or proprioception, but compared to gender dysphoria, which located the tension I observed in you in your choice of clothes or friends, these ideas offered a paradigm that addressed your physicality.

With Leslie's help, we learned to use engine planning to approach stressful situations. We started to anticipate circumstances that were likely to trigger your anxiety or devolve into boredom. You started new activities like playing the drums and rock climbing, which gave your body lots of big inputs. Leslie's office became a place where you learned how to manage your energy and moods. Our family made progress. You started to sleep better, and your explosive quality evened out. The slamwhams began to abate. Generally, your system began to feel more organized, which let the family settle into a smoother phase.

Watching those videos was one of the first times I felt myself let go of something. Belly-heaving, rib-cracking laughter jostled free a weight I had not known I had been carrying. When psychologists first suggested you might have gender dysphoria, I girded myself against an entire worldview—diagnosis and medical treatment—that felt scary and that I know now I didn't completely understand. I kept myself together with a vice-like grip. I was committed to celebrating you, but I was also terrified of what

I was being told supporting you meant. I pressed my fear down so hard it practically fused into my bones. Then, suddenly, at that dinner, all that laughing kicked that tight hold loose.

Even though we still don't know what to do about your fertility, I can see your future. I know that what I observed all those years ago in your body was sensory in nature and probably related to your gender. And I know now that keeping your body aligned with your identity through hormone therapy will support you. Laughing together about how it looked to me back then let me forgive myself for what I had failed to see, and I was, for a minute at least, able to let go. I felt lighter than I had in years.

REFLECTION QUESTIONS

- How often do you take time off from stressful parenting issues to celebrate what is good about your child and your family? What in your life can you point to and say, there is more right with us than wrong with us? What does it feel like to consider your child's future and ask yourself, how good could it be?
- The future is, by definition, always unknown and therefore uncertain. What future dreams do you have for your family? What would it be like to give yourself a few minutes a day to imagine a happy future for your child and for your family? What small actions can you take right now to move the tiniest bit in the direction of that happy future? What joyful moment could you have with your child today to remind yourself of what is going well?

Letter 14

October 2019: History in the Making

I needed to see Aimee Stephens' case argued in front of the Supreme Court for myself. I wanted to lay my own eyes on the nine justices whose opinions would indelibly mark the path of your future, to see their faces, to hear the exact words they spoke, and the tone in which they spoke them. Whatever came of the case, I didn't want to get a filtered-down version of what happened. I wanted to draw my own conclusions.

Aimee Stephens was a 58-year-old trans woman born in Fayetteville, North Carolina (the same town where Dad was born). She was assigned male at birth and lived that way for most of her life. She married her wife, Donna, and worked as funeral director in Detroit before understanding she was transgender. For many years she battled an ongoing depression. While working for R.G. & G.R. Harris Funeral Home, her gender identity came into focus and was identified as a root cause of her long-term depression. After testing the waters at her workplace by sharing her story with a few supportive colleagues, she decided to come out in a letter to her boss.

When I first read the letter, something about it reminded me of a generous quality I've seen in you. She forgave her co-workers in advance for what they might not understand (although other people's ignorance was not her responsibility); she told her story plainly without covering herself with any kind of protection (although, like everyone else, Aimee Stephens had the right to privacy), and she made clear she did not want a revolution (although she deserved one), or even a revision of gendered expectations around attire; she simply wanted to be recognized for who she understood herself to be, and to keep the job she had been doing well for many years.

I've witnessed you struggle and then extend the same magnanimity to people—to classmates and adults who mistreat or misunderstand you, to the security guard at the airport who wanted to know why you had to think for a second about your name, to the family friend who came to our house and mis-gendered you over and over again. It's a quality I admire, but that lately also makes me nervous. It is your natural way, but it contributes to the sense that I've really not prepared you for the world as it is.

Aimee Stephens was fired two weeks after her boss received her letter. As I write down her story for you, I want you to know that real love does not require us to be agreeable or to avoid conflict. There is no love without justice. And if you ever find yourself angry or frustrated, know that justified anger exists. Loving, heart-fueled anger can arise to demand mutuality and respect for common humanity. Aimee Stephens understood this. She was generous with her community, and then, when they failed to return her generosity, she took an impassioned stand for her rights. She is a good role model for you.

As of this fall, California is one of only twenty-three states in the country that offers trans people legal protection from discrimination.* Twenty-one out of fifty. In over half of the states in this country a trans person's employment can be terminated just because their boss doesn't like trans people. This isn't a perfect comparison, but it's like we are living in a new kind of Jim Crow era. The nature of our democracy means that your human rights can be radically different from state to state. The Civil Rights Act that was passed by Congress in 1964 is one way our country has tried to bolster the rights of citizens across the country, and Aimee Stephens's case is asking whether that law protects gay and transgender citizens.

The atmosphere in DC was uncomfortable. The day I arrived I took a walk along the Potomac River. Three dark helicopters flew low overhead, in a tight formation. Their engines thudded the air so hard and so close I felt it in the back of my skull, along my spine and in my actual hip sockets. A woman walking alongside me saw how startled I was and explained that the group of choppers always flew together to conceal the president, who flew in Marine One, one of the three. The booming and thumping felt like danger bearing down on me. The feeling only increased the next day at court.

I arrived at the Supreme Court just before dawn; the sidewalk was still wet from rain the night before. Standing in the cold, I wound my wool scarf one more time around my neck and bundled my jacket close. My fellow citizens in line included a computer engineer who worked at Google (he didn't know Dad), a patent attorney, an entourage dressed in black who looked like they might be from the funeral home, and a bunch of students.

* For the latest figures, see www.lgbtmap.org/equality-maps/non_discrimination_laws

The students had been camping out for days, sleeping on the sidewalk, even in the rain. Those of us who were able to afford it had hired professional line waiters to hold our place (it seemed to me more than half the people at the front of the line had done this) and had arrived early the day of the case to relieve our proxies. A man sat at the head of the line under a rainbow umbrella. He had become our informal team leader, writing our names down, holding spots if people had to go to the bathroom, and periodically filming himself with an iPhone set up on a tripod.

Around 8:00 am a court officer handed each of the first 50 of us an orange slip of paper that looked like it just rolled off someone's old desktop printer. A line drawing of the goddess Themis, the goddess of justice, appeared to the left of a few lines of text: Supreme Court of the United States, Admission Card. Mine was marked #40.

With our orange papers in hand, we shuffled single file past the metal fences set out to control protesters who were expected later in the day. We walked across the stone field of the marble plaza. It blazed white as the sun rose in front of the court's facade. Our line flanked the huge austere building and passed under its imposing pediment, where the phrase, "Equal Justice Under Law," was inscribed in the stone overhead.

When I was in college, I had visited the Supreme Court and had passed under those very same stone words. As a young woman I felt elevated by the lofty guarantees of my American citizenship. But standing in the very same place the day of Aimee Stephens' case, I shivered and did my best not to think about the precarious stakes of the day. In the damp morning, on the precipice of a few hours that were either going to affirm or deny your rights, I spent most of my energy wondering about the possibility of a cup of coffee. The fragrant steam, the barky familiar taste, the velvet splash of cream. It was early still, not quite nine o'clock, and the case would begin at ten. Maybe there would be a cafe inside and maybe inside the cafe there would be coffee. I hunched my shoulders against the cold and rubbed my palms together as if I could conjure luck in the form of a hot cup.

After crossing the threshold of the building and passing through the first security line, the scale of the architecture changed. If the exterior looked like a sacred temple, its corridors reminded me of the old Palo Alto Post Office. The aged granite floor, the echoing hallways, the institutional fluorescent lighting bouncing off dirty white walls thick with many years of repainting, the dusty smell. Small day lockers required a single quarter to lock up personal items, as required by the court.

After waiting in line in a hallway for half an hour, the court officer deposited us in the Supreme Court cafeteria. Here was the cup of coffee I had hoped for. I made my way to the tall black carafes lined up on the counter. I pumped myself a large cup and paid in cash. I sat down at a long wooden table alongside the huddle of people I had gotten to know waiting in line. The coffee tasted like it had been brewed for days, the bitterness concentrated and sharp. It was the worst cup of coffee I'd ever had, and I thought of throwing it out, but held on to it anyway, to warm my hands.

I thought of you when I saw a group of teenagers sitting across the dining hall from me. They had been the last four people in line to receive orange tickets for the day, and I decided to go over and talk to them. Crossing the room, I saw Justice Sotomayor out of the corner of my eye. She was checking out at the cash register with two cups of that terrible coffee. I noticed that she chatted with the woman working the register and seemed to know her name. I felt like I had just seen Wonder Woman walk through the Hall of Justice and wondered if the teenagers felt the same.

The students looked impossibly young. One of them wore a red Liberty University sweatshirt,* so I knew ahead of time that we did not share the same opinions. I guess it was their youth that attracted me to them. Their gumption to get into court impressed me, and they looked so much like you and your friends that I felt unexpectedly maternal toward them. I introduced myself and asked them where they were from (Virginia). They told me about their homeschooling program. One of them did most of the talking while the other three watched with anxious interest, looking as if they expected our conversation to eventually go poorly. I was surprised how easily the five of us slipped into familiar roles—me, the mom chaperone, and the four teens, a group of bright, spunky kids on an incredible field trip.

When I asked what brought them to court that day, the most vocal boy told me they were there because they believed that "God made people male and female." The facts they had about transgender people were contrary to both the facts we know and the experience we have lived firsthand. One of the students had met a transgender person once, but none had ever had the opportunity to get to know someone who was trans. Our conversation stayed genial, because I didn't want to enter a debate with them. The short time we had together was alive with mutual, albeit fragile, possibility. And as if I were starting a campfire with flint, when sparks of possibility appeared, my greatest instinct was to coax the flame.

* A private evangelical Christian university in Lynchburg, Virginia.

Our conversation came to a pause when court officers arrived in the cafeteria to move us to our next security checkpoint. While in line, a few of us realized we needed to stash one or two last items in the lockers. The only girl from the group of high school students found herself in the ladies' room with me, looking for a place to store her jacket, but without the quarter she needed to pay for a locker. I let her stuff it in with mine, just like I would have if any of your friends were stuck in a jam. I didn't think twice about what news channel she watched or whether she understood gender the way we do. The small locker room was buzzing with activity and I'm sure the girl had no idea how many trans women surrounded her right then. Our relationship was fleeting but respectful.

I could not help but wonder what it would have been like if she had met you that day. I'm sure she and her friends would have liked you. You would have told them a joke or shown them a meme about cats on your phone, and they would have laughed. It was easy to envision you all getting along (and using the gender-assigned bathrooms), because I had seen it happen so many times before. The young woman and I rushed out of the locker room and back into line before passing through the final security check point together. Once in the courtroom, she took a seat with her friends on the other side of the room from me.

The courtroom where oral arguments are heard at the Supreme Court is as grand as the courthouse edifice. The ceiling soars and the justices' bench sits high up on a dais in the front of the tallest set of red velvet curtains I have ever seen. The court session seemed close to beginning when a couple of ordinary-looking people slipped out from behind the red velvet curtains like stagehands. Items were placed at the justices' seats.

A spiral notebook, a manila folder. A large gray coffee mug at one end of the bench, a metal travel mug at one of the middle seats. I suspected these were clerks prepping their justice's desk for the court day. Shortly after they disappeared behind the red curtain, a loud buzzer sounded. A court officer bellowed, "All rise!"

I jumped to my feet at the sound of the buzzer. Then the justices floated out from behind the red curtain like gods in black robes. They stood at their seats with all the gravitas endowed to their role. Then they sat in unison. As if to break the spell, Justice Gorsuch yawned a wide-open bearish yawn. Then he lifted his big gray coffee mug to his lips. That he looked like my own granddad gave me a warm feeling. I wondered if he was drinking the same bad bitter coffee I had just thrown into the trash.

Justice Ginsburg, our family hero, and your school's designated change-maker for the school year, was wearing a bright-red beaded necklace. She was so small behind the bench that I was barely able to see her above the horizon of the giant desk. She must have been two heads shorter than her colleagues. Justice Kavanaugh sat in the last seat at the far-right end of the bench. His face merged so easily with college boys I had known, boys who drank hard and made off-color jokes, who belonged to the Harvard finals clubs that their fathers belonged to, who played lacrosse or hockey, boys who asked me for my notes in chemistry, in econ, in American lit. Boys who assumed they worked as hard as the rest of us, but never did. Perhaps it was an unfair characterization, but I can't pretend to be objective about him.

David Cole, the legal director from the ACLU, was Aimee Stephens' lead counsel and made the first opening argument. He had not spoken for more than a couple of minutes when Chief Justice Roberts interrupted him with the question of the morning: "If the objection of a transgender man transitioning to woman is that he should be allowed to use he or she, should be allowed to use the women's bathroom, now how do you analyze that?" His tone was pointed, almost aggressive, as if to say, *Look, here is the obvious problem—we cannot have men in the women's room.* His confidence contrasted with the way he stumbled over the terms. It was clear he didn't have a firm grasp on how to identify someone who had been born male bodied and who grew up to be a woman. The question was so clumsy and ignorant, it made my heart sink. It was dispiriting to have come to the highest court in the land only to be confronted with a chief justice who did not seem to have mastered the basic vocabulary. The courtroom was filled with trans attorneys that day, and I couldn't help but imagine what the moment felt like from their perspective. So far, the day in court did not seem to be going very well.

Later the lead counsel for the funeral home proposed a hypothetical scenario in which an imagined trans woman was hired to work at an overnight shelter as a "counselor to women who have been raped, trafficked, and abused." He made prurient, sensational inferences about what it meant to force victimized women to share facilities with a trans woman. I had not anticipated the defense would work so hard to gin up disgust, when the real question was whether Aimee Stephens deserved to be fired for being trans.

In the face of what seemed to me to be overt bigotry, I understood at that moment that no matter how the case was decided, there would always be people who favored views like these. No court decision, however positive, would have the power to transform the hearts of the most extreme Americans. Whether Aimee Stephens won or lost her case, you would always need a safe person-to-person network to travel confidently across the country.

An image came to mind of an event Nonny had taken me to when I was in middle school called Hands Across America. We had joined a human chain to raise money to support homeless and food-insecure families in the USA. It was a hot day, and the crowd of people was packed onto the West Side Highway. Music played, bodies swayed, and everyone held hands. The energy felt like a current running through my fingertips. I was a single cell in a living wire that was more than 4000 miles long. The repetition of a simple linkage, one palm in the hand of another, over and over and over again, felt powerful. In court that day I made a wish for something like that for you, but not just a single chain. I wanted an entire web of linkages that connected you to your whole country.

Towards the end of the oral arguments, I felt glad that I hadn't brought you with me. It would have been terrible for you to hear the hypotheticals in the halls of the highest court in the land. I felt so anxious toward the end of the session that I almost missed the most hopeful turn in the case. Justice Gorsuch admitted that the text of the Civil Rights Act of 1964 was written in such a way that it was very close to protecting the rights of the trans community, but the question he wanted David Cole to answer was whether or not protecting trans people from employment discrimination was judicial overstep, considering there was no way that legislators in 1964 could have anticipated the law being used to protect trans people. Justice Gorsuch wanted to know whether the court should take into consideration "the massive social upheaval" that would be caused by interpreting the law in Stephens' favor. Cole's response was the high point of the day.

He pointed out that federal courts of appeals had been recognizing that discrimination against trans people was sex discrimination for 20 years. Then he did something brilliant; he recognized the trans attorneys who were in the courtroom that day. He pointed out that there were trans male lawyers in the courtroom following the men's dress code and using the men's restroom—and that there had been no upheaval at all at the court that day. Then he described the millions of trans employees who showed up peacefully at their jobs every day. His argument shot down every hypothetical suggestion in one point. He was calling out the truth, and everyone in court that day knew it.

As I walked out of the courthouse after the oral arguments, I passed Aimee Stephens sitting proudly in her chair. Attorneys and reporters made an entourage around her. I followed behind them, and when we entered the bright daylight, we encountered throngs of protesters pressed up against the metal fence. They waved flags and chanted for Aimee, "We-love-you. We-love-you. We-love-you." A large group of people sat in the middle of the street waiting to be arrested. Police officers in bullet-proof vests zip-tied the protesters' wrists and loaded them into buses to take them down to the police station. I called home to tell Dad I was fine, and then made my way back to the hotel, where I sat down at the bar and ordered a Manhattan, and then another. When I got to my hotel room, I cleared my calendar for the next two days so that when I got home I could tackle your identity paperwork right away.

REFLECTION QUESTIONS

- As families we are living through an epic inflection point in the history of human gender. How does considering this larger context impact your own experience? What is intimidating about this moment? What is empowering about this moment? What other historical movements could you turn to for inspiration (for example, the Women's Rights Movement, the Civil Rights Movement, the movement for Climate Conservation and Justice)?

- What radical social changes have you lived through in your lifetime? How can previous patterns of social progress help you feel connected to community, supported, and part of something bigger?
- What is one organization you can reach out to connect with communities who are committed to progress that will support your child?

Interview

Shannon Minter on Looking Back and Looking Forward in the Fight for Trans Rights

Shannon Minter is Legal Director of the National Center for Lesbian Rights (NCLR),* one of the nation's leading advocacy organizations for lesbian, gay, bisexual, and transgender people. Shannon was lead counsel for same-sex couples in the landmark California marriage equality case, which held that same-sex couples have the fundamental right to marry, and that laws that discriminate based on sexual orientation are inherently discriminatory and subject to the highest level of constitutional scrutiny. Shannon was also NCLR's lead attorney in *Christian Legal Society v. Martinez*, a US Supreme Court decision upholding student group policies prohibiting discrimination based on sexual orientation and gender identity, and rejecting the argument that such policies violated a student group's rights to freedom of speech, religion, and association. NCLR represented Hastings Outlaw, an LGBTQ student group that intervened to help defend the nondiscrimination policy.

Cristina: Shannon, can you start us off with some background

* www.nclrights.org

about how you became involved in advocating for trans supportive laws, and give us a little history that was leading up to the Bostock case (Bostock v. Clayton County, 590 US)?

Shannon: I'm 61 and I was born in 1961. I grew up in the sixties and seventies. And it was great being a tomboy up until puberty. And then after puberty, it was no longer a viable social option. So it was rough. I went through a lot of a lot of the terrible struggles that so many LGBTQ kids go through. And too many are still going through the same stuff, but it's so much better now. I am thinking specifically of the harassment, and how my own parents rejected me only because they just didn't know what to do. They did what we now know from some of the Family Acceptance Project® research* is sort of the worst thing to do, out of misguided love for me. They were just so desperate for me not to grow up to be lesbian. I don't even think transgender was in anyone's mind. And so, they did everything they could to try to discourage me—isolating me, shaming me—all the things that we now know you're not supposed to do. It was really rough. And it was scary. When I was in high school I was physically attacked by classmates, and I would lie awake at night afraid for my safety.

But the other painful thing was I just did not know what was going on with myself. I did think that I knew I was attracted to girls. I was assigned female at birth. And I thought, well, I must be a lesbian. But that was the beginning, the only idea I had words for. I almost see it as an equally damaging trauma to not have any ability to know anything about transgender identity or people.

I didn't get a real sense of what was going on with me until

* https://familyproject.sfsu.edu

I got involved in HIV advocacy. It was such a fantastic relief to me when I did finally learn about transgender people. And that was a process for me, it wasn't like I immediately felt I must be transgender. I kind of went through what our society has gone through, and what people often do go through, which included processing my own negative reactions. At first, I felt like that seems really wrong and bizarre, and scary. And I did not have any kind of conscious identification. Although looking back, I can see it was a topic of great interest to me. I had first become aware of transgender women, but it wasn't until I saw a film called *Female Misbehavior* that I saw the possibility of being a transgender man. I just couldn't stop thinking about that film. But even then I didn't put it together. I had a girlfriend at the time who said to me, gosh, when I wouldn't shut up about it. Gosh, you think maybe you're transgender and I was like, for Pete's sake, don't you think I'd know if I was?

But to make a long story short, I eventually moved to San Francisco and went to work for the National Center for Lesbian Rights. There could not have been a better place for someone who was about to come out as transgender than San Francisco. I'm grateful that San Francisco already had anti-discrimination laws and a health clinic, which is where I went to get my care when I figured it out. But I started to meet transgender men, and especially Jamison Green, who's such a hero in the movement. And he was so good to me. I don't know how many other trans men have transitioned because of James. But his support really did it for me. And then I did realize, wow, this is what has been the mystery all along.

If there's a dividing point in my life between the misery that was me before and the real joy that was being me since, it's my transition. It is just so wonderful to feel good about being in this body, and to have others see me the same way I see myself. And to not carry that constant agony around thinking "This is wrong, I am wrong. So everything's wrong." I couldn't even look people in the eye before I transitioned. It was awful. But now, I am just feeling normal and not having to think about myself all the time. That's the blessing of it.

I transitioned in the mid-nineteen-nineties. The really cool thing was that I happened to be in the right place at the right time in the right job working for one of the national LGBT groups to get to be part of the incredible legal trajectory that transgender rights has been on. The speed in which things have changed is almost unprecedented in our movement, I cannot think of another movement within the larger queer world that has moved as quickly. Maybe HIV advocacy would be comparable. But for the trans community there was just so much energy and so much change in such a short period of time. And to be part of that was exhilarating and so much fun.

In the mid-nineteen-nineties almost no courts had ever ruled in favor of a transgender person. There were a few outliers. Renée Richardson, one transgender tennis player, had won a sex discrimination case in the late seventies confirming her right to play women's tennis. There were some decisions holding that transgender people do have a right to medical care under certain federal governmental medical programs. So, there was a little bit to work with. But there were a lot more negative decisions where federal courts and state courts mostly left transgender plaintiffs out of court, ridiculing their claims, and talking about transgender people in openly disparaging terms. There's one case where a judge compared a transgender woman to the Shakespeare character who thought he had turned into a donkey. And like I said, there were no broad anti-discrimination laws. Minnesota passed the first state law protecting transgender people in 1985. And that was thanks to some transgender advocates in that state who happened to be connected to the political infrastructure. The gay rights movement had not embraced transgender people or issues at all. So, to go from that moment, to where we are now with the Bostock decision, has been amazing. And to get to be a part of that has been thrilling.

Now we've got the Supreme Court affirming transgender people's civil rights nationwide, of course, and the LGBT movement is now fully inclusive. And transgender people have many, many state and federal protections. So yes, we're in a different world, and the social acceptance is off the charts. It is so much better. Trans kids who are being born now don't have to go through decades of confusion and uncertainty and rejection and without access medical care, not being able to be who they are. It's a great thing.

We were able to change things so fast because the grassroots movement spread like wildfire with groups of transgender people organizing at the local level. It was democracy in action. There were so many groups, so many people pushing local ordinances. There was a group called It's Time America, and they had chapters all over the place. Phyllis Frey, who was the first trans person to be a judge in our whole country from Texas, of all places, started organizing this international transgender rights conference, which she just funded out of her own pocket and single-handedly organized for a number of years. That was revolutionary. That's where I met so many other transgender lawyers. So many of us first met each other and started to form networks of legal advocates at the conferences.

Cristina: During that time, what kinds of laws were being passed?

Shannon: Basic laws that added transgender people to local laws that prohibit discrimination on other bases, usually like sex, race, religion, and so forth. In other words: local human rights laws. And that's how we built protections—by starting at the local level, and then you get enough municipalities to build a foundation to get your state legislature to pass a law. That's what groups do, and transgender people did it in record time.

At the same time, we were trying to get all those laws passed there was a real renaissance in bringing cases to court. But mostly what changed as that political movement took shape was the cultural moment. There was a *Time* magazine cover, which happens every so often, and I think cultural influences have helped courts to view transgender people more positively. Leading up to Bostock, that's the really the big thing that changed, more so than our legal arguments. Because we'd always had the basic legal argument that if a person is discriminated against because they're transgender, because they've changed their sex, because they were identified as one sex at birth, and now they're identified as the other sex. Then that's about sex, that's gender discrimination, plain and simple. And if you're against them, because you think a transgender woman doesn't meet your idea of what a woman should be, should act like, or look like—well, that's gender stereotyping. So, the legal arguments were always incredibly straightforward. They were really the same arguments that have been presented to the courts in the seventies and eighties and early nineties. And if you go back and look at those decisions from that time period, it's not as though courts engaged in some extended analysis to reject them. They really were just like: are you kidding me? You're transgender, and the law was never intended to protect you.

We were making the same arguments, but the courts were taking them more seriously because they take transgender people more seriously and it was harder just to dismiss them. And then there was important change surrounding decisions involving sex discrimination generally. For example, a case in which the court found that men were protected from being sexually harassed by other men. That was a big deal because the court said, hey, it doesn't matter that Congress wasn't thinking about that when they enacted Title VII, the law that prohibits sex discrimination in the workplace. And prohibiting sexual harassment between men is a reasonable application of the law. This decision firmly established that Title VII could apply to issues beyond the problems Congress had in mind when they enacted the statute. The court was willing to consider the language of the law, its broad purpose, and its reasonable application in other contexts, not just the original specific contest of when the statute was originally passed.

For the Bostock case we were able to say, yes, it doesn't matter whether Congress passed Title VII because they had a desire to protect transgender people. They probably weren't thinking about transgender people at all. Maybe some of them were, but most weren't. But that's okay. Because that's not how you apply the law in other contexts. And then there was another important series of decisions, including this very famous Price Waterhouse decision, when the precedent was set that Title VII protected against stereotyping. It's true that when Congress first passed Title VII, the concept of a sex stereotype was not really a thing, it wasn't a prominent part of the general discourse, and it was zero part of legal discourse. It simply didn't exist as a legal concept until the Price Waterhouse case. So, you can see all this just builds to a kind of a crescendo to Bostock. By the time we got to the Supreme Court hearing the Bostock case, there had been a good 20 years of federal courts almost uniformly agreeing that yes, if a person's employers discriminate against them because they're transgender, that's about that person's gender. And that's prohibited by law. So, the scary thing about Bostock was the fear that all that precedent would all be swept away.

I was very worried about that. It would have been utterly devastating—a setback of monumental proportions. And that day was just terrifying. The big thing that was not encouraging me in court that day was that even the more progressive justices were saying things that seemed to evidence a lack of familiarity and overall misinformation about transgender people. And that was very concerning. I will say Justice Ginsburg was a bright spot that day. Thank goodness she was still on the court. I am sure that her presence on the court for that decision made a huge—perhaps definitive—difference given that Justice Gorsuch, a very conservative justice, wrote the opinion. In the end, that he was joined by Chief Justice Roberts was just amazing.

It still seems to be nothing short of miraculous that we won given the make-up of the Supreme Court. I do think Justice Ginsburg was clearly the one justice up there who fully and completely and entirely and with enormous clarity understood the issues and what was at stake. She must have persuaded those other justices that a mess on Bostock was going to undo decades of progress in equality law.

Bostock is the capstone of all the progress that the trans community has made over the course of 20 years, and it has launched a new positive era in the law for transgender people. I think it's also made a big cultural difference. To have the Supreme Court rule in favor of transgender people means a lot. The court still does carry a lot of weight with the public, so it's been wonderful. And legally, of course, it has opened the door to a lot of positive federal agency policies. And those have been followed as well by a lot of states that kind of track what the federal government does. There's a whole slew of new positive court decisions—in housing, education, and healthcare, All we have to do now to resolve these cases is quote that sentence from the opinion stating that discrimination because a person's transgender is necessarily discrimination because of sex. It's a powerful decision that has completely, and I hope forever, changed the place of transgender people in our society.

Cristina: What do you think about these state laws that are making things so difficult for transgender youth with sports and medical treatment for kids? Will these be deemed discrimination in the highest courts of the land? It's not your first rodeo, but as a parent of a trans kiddo, it is my first rodeo, and I feel like I was just about to exhale, and now I'm freaking out again.

Shannon: We're going to be okay. We really are. For one thing, let's not forget that these deeply anti-LGBTQ groups can be very effective and smart. They hit us with an unexpected campaign targeting trans kids and focusing on mostly sports, but to some degree, also medical care. In one year, we suddenly got, like, 40 some laws that were all virtually identical. Clearly, it's an orchestrated campaign. This wasn't some kind of spontaneous thing that independently happened. But I think we did pretty darn well. We stopped most of them, but not all of them. Now you have a couple of those state laws about medical care that have slipped through and passed. And that's more than I'd like. But it could have been so much worse. Given that we had no time to mount a response. We just did it. People leaped into the breach, and I think we did a tremendous job of countering the tsunami of misinformation that came along with this campaign. We should feel good about that. We have to keep that up. We've had really good success challenging these laws in court already. We need to continue to be careful and strategic, but so far we have been very successful fighting these laws.

In the long run, this will ultimately be to our benefit. It will never make up for the kids that are getting hurt now, don't get me wrong. But this process of fighting the backlash in court will advance public understanding of these issues enormously. If you think about it, the other side, the bad guys that don't want to see transgender people have any protection or rights or acceptance—they just funded a multibillion-dollar public education campaign for us, they have injected these issues into the public arena. I mean, do you know how hard it is to get attention on anything? And so now we have to do our part. We have this opportunity handed to us on a platter, and we need to continue to educate people and advance our arguments, which we are already doing.

Letter 15
October 2019: Identity

While I was in Washington, the county court order to change your name and gender marker on your birth certificate arrived. It looked like nothing in the pile of regular mail, a nondescript white envelope anyone could have missed. But after what I witnessed at the Supreme Court it felt like a magic key in my hand. Inside the envelope your old birth certificate was stapled to the new paperwork. We needed this precious bundle to fill out one more set of forms requesting a revised birth certificate with your male name and the correct gender marker on it from the California Department of Health Records.

I started the process of changing your legal identity after Roger Severino, Director of the Office for Civil Rights at the Department of Health and Human Services who was appointed by Donald Trump, had issued new religious conscience rules in healthcare as part of his mission to ensure that government policy did not "radically re-define 'sex.'" Along with what I had learned from Elizabeth Gill at the ACLU, I feared the right to change your name and gender marker on your documents (a right that you have in California, but that trans people in other states do not have) might disappear. This feeling has felt more intense while the Aimee Stephens case remains undecided.

So last week, I went to the San Mateo County Courthouse in Redwood City. I actually ended up going three times before successfully submitting the petition to change your name and gender identity on your birth certificate. The first time I went to the courthouse I learned I had completed one of the six forms incorrectly. The next time I found out I needed an extra copy of your birth certificate, as well as a self-addressed stamped envelope and a seventh form that had not appeared in the list online. Once I made it through that gauntlet, there was the shock of the cost: $435. When I finally heard the thunk-thunk-thunk of official rubber stamps pounding your paperwork, I had to restrain myself from throwing victory fists into the air in the middle of the quiet county office.

Those rubber stamps were soldiers in the army of bureaucracy. There were so many in the county clerk's office that I took a picture of them balanced in one long row on a precipice between two office cubicles. That it was 2019 in Silicon Valley and this army of Luddite tools stood between you and the official documents you needed to stay safe seemed impossible to me. I thought of the gay couple in Rowan County, Kentucky, who had been denied access to a marriage license by a county clerk with a rubber stamp. Sometimes when I think about the precarity of your rights I feel like I don't know what country we live in anymore.

I felt so relieved when the clerk accepted your paperwork. He congratulated me and told me that your new birth certificate would arrive in about a month. This means that when you get your driver's license, when you take your SATs, when you leave home for college, the paper trail that makes up an American life will be marked as male and will not out you. You will be so much more in control of your identity than you would be if we wait until you turn 18 to do this. I left the courthouse, texted "WOOT" to a few different friends, and drove home with the windows of the minivan rolled all the way down, my radio blaring "Don't Stop Believin'" by Journey.

Letter 16
November 2019: Options

A phone call I had with a college classmate has changed everything for you. I called her to interview her about a book she has coming out, but just as we were about to hang up, I asked how her trans son was doing. We traded some mom stories, and then I asked if she was open to discussing a more personal topic. I wanted to know if she had been thinking at all about her son's fertility. Not only had she been thinking about it, but she also reported that her son had successfully retrieved egg follicles and stored them for the future.

"Wait, so your son was okay going off his blockers?" I asked.

"No. That would have been way too much for him. Turns out he didn't have to," she said, and then explained the round of hormone injections her son did to grow mature follicles and then retrieve them. No doctor I could recall had suggested a trans boy could stay on his blockers and retrieve eggs. My friend explained that she thought the procedure was rare and not without risk. Her own son had experienced some symptoms of ovarian hyperstimulation syndrome. I did not know what that was or how dangerous it was, but when I asked her if he would do it again, she said yes. She was not happy that he had experienced a more extreme version of the procedure than might have been necessary (I looked it up online—it can be fatal, so it's not a negligible risk), but she said her son felt that he had done something for his future that he felt good about. "Ten days is a short time to make way for an entire future," is how she put it. I hung up the phone and immediately texted Dad. He was excited, but not quite as much as I was. It was as if he had the idea that I was going to track down a solution and this discovery was just fulfilled his assumption.

I insisted he join us for the consultation with Dr. Kim, the reproductive endocrinologist I had met at Gender Spectrum. Generally, Dad and I have been on the same page about your healthcare, and I usually did not ask him to take time off work to go with us to appointments. But I didn't want to miss any crucial new information at this one. Over the years I had learned that processing new information about your fertility was stressful for me, and I quickly felt flooded. If Dad were there in person, I felt like we would be better able to shoulder the burden of decision making as a team.

Dr. Kim's office was on the sixth floor of a building at the brand-new UCSF hospital campus, overlooking San Francisco Bay. A bulldozer rolled back and forth in front of the entrance, smoothing a fresh layer of asphalt on the street. When we checked in at the front desk, the receptionist asked for my name, and I quickly realized the office staff assumed I was the patient. Although Dr. Kim handled pediatric reproductive endocrinology, it was still relatively unusual to see a child in the office. A healthy pre-teen boy was an especially unlikely patient.

We were taken to an exam room, an unpleasant surprise since I told you we had scheduled a consultation. "I thought you said this was only talking?" you asked as the nurse approached me with a blood pressure cuff. "I'm not the patient," I said. She rechecked her chart, looked around the room as if taking a head count, then took your blood pressure and left. I promised if she tried to take any more measurements, I'd stop her. She returned shortly after she had disappeared and ushered us into Dr. Kim's small office.

You, Dad, and I sat in three chairs squeezed together in front of the doctor's desk. On the other side of it, she sat at her desk with an intern hovering over her. All together there were five of us jammed into a bright room that was hardly big enough for two people. Despite the rocky start to our visit, it was good to see Dr. Kim's friendly face again. She introduced herself to you and Dad. Then introduced her intern and asked if it was okay for her to join us since our meeting was such a special appointment. It felt uncomfortable, like we were a specimen family, but we also did not say no. She asked how old you were and how long you had been on blockers. Then she asked how you felt about starting testosterone. You said, "I'd start tomorrow if I could," and then explained that you'd start in a few months, when you turned 14.

"But you are interested in doing egg retrieval, right?" she asked. You looked at me, and I nodded. We at least wanted the information. She explained the procedure and then said, "But you'd have to go off your blockers to do it." You looked at me. This wasn't what I had told you. It wasn't what my friend had told me. I interrupted her. "Wait, does he have to go off the blockers?" She explained that the blockers had to be stopped for the oocytes to mature properly. I cocked my head, confused. I had assumed she would have learned about advancements in her field before I did.

It was not like we lived in a small town off the grid of progress. Dr. Kim was a leading reproductive endocrinologist in the epicenter of the gender-diverse universe.

I told her about my college classmate's son. "I'm pretty sure they did not have to go off blockers," I explained. And Dr. Kim stared at me "Really? Are you sure?" she asked. I could tell she was as surprised as I was about which of us had the newer information. She asked me for the name of the doctor who did the procedure.

"Michah Hill," she repeated his name. "I know him, I mean I don't *know him* know him. But I know his work. I'm surprised he didn't publish this case." She wrote a note to herself to call him during the week, remarking that if what I was saying was true, it was real news and should have been published. She promised to call me as soon as she heard from him directly.

Sitting in her office I felt like I was caught in a falling elevator with no brakes. My stomach flew into my throat. Is this what your future came down to? The dumb luck of a phone call I happened to have? In the past, I might have experienced this moment cinematically, as if we were the luckiest of the lucky, standing in a special ray of golden light that somehow brought us together with just the information and people we needed at just the right moment. Instead, my new awareness about life at the margins of American culture made me skeptical. Finding the best healthcare for you felt maddeningly random, as if your life were a roulette ball clattering in a circle toward any old number.

It was hard for me to stay focused, but there was more we had to get through that morning. I changed the topic to ovarian extraction, the procedure that had been done for the mother whose photograph I had seen at Gender Spectrum. Dr. Kim explained that, in her reproductive endocrinology practice, she saw most of the group's pediatric cases. Most were girls with cancer, like the young mother in the photograph had been. After doing the work for a few years, she wondered why she didn't see more trans children coming through. She was happy we had come in to see her. And although my stomach hadn't totally recovered from the shock, I was happy to have met a doctor who was curious about cases like yours.

I asked Dr. Kim if she ever performed ovarian extraction. She told me that she did—sometimes she extracted a little bit of ovarian tissue, and sometimes the whole ovary. In my research I had learned that the freezing of ovarian tissue was a specialized procedure that required a very specific kind of freezer. I had read there were only a few in the USA. Dr. Kim confirmed that UCSF was one of the few research centers that housed one. In fact, the freezing of ovarian tissue was so new, so experimental, that it was all but free for patients to store their ovaries in the freezer at UCSF because there was a research grant helping pay for the procedure so that scientists could learn more about doing it successfully.

So here it was. We had found our way to the plated glass building just off the 101 where someone had been thinking about the science required to preserve your fertility. Although the appointment had been a rollercoaster, we had located the innovator who was looking toward the horizon of your future.

As we finished up with Dr. Kim, Dad said, "So we have some real options." He was excited. We had not had much time before the appointment to catch up on what I was learning, and this was so much more promising than what he had expected.

"Yes. They're all pretty experimental, but worth thinking about, especially if the case Cristina mentioned turns out to be a good model for us," she replied.

After we left, Dad threw me a fist bump, and while we waited for the elevator, he complimented me.

"You were awesome in there. Jake, did you see that? Mom rocked it."

I mumbled thanks and watched the light of the floor indicator switch numbers. I didn't have it in me to talk and was holding back tears that I didn't understand. The appointment had gone well. Dr. Kim couldn't have been nicer. I even felt like we were going to get good news from the doctor at Walter Reed Medical Center. Later, sitting in my office, I realized that knowing more than your reproductive endocrinologist rattled me. I was not the expert. I *needed* experts to guide our family in your care. The randomness of the distribution of new information made me feel vulnerable in a way I rarely felt.

I felt the same way when Chief Justice Roberts stumbled over the appropriate words to use for a trans woman at the Supreme Court. In both cases, I sought institutional authority in the fields that were about to impact you. And they let me down—at least if their power was supposed to come from knowing more than I did. Dad was so proud of me for having discovered the cutting-edge information I brought to that meeting, and I wished I could feel the same. Instead, I just wanted to curl up in a ball under my desk to hide from a context that felt capricious and only accidentally under control. Which, in practical terms, felt like no control at all.

Standing on the sidewalk in the sun-filled canyon between the Zuckerberg building and Benioff Children's Hospital, you said you wanted boba tea. "I think we need to do something to celebrate making it through that appointment," you said. I could not have agreed more.

In the car, Dad chatted about all the options you had. He

and I were in different mental spaces, which felt exhausting to me. Where he heard that you had options, I heard that you were going to be part of version 1.0 of fertility preservation, not even 1.0, more like beta. And I was tired of living on the bleeding edge all the time. I didn't even like updating my iPhone. The updates improved some features, but always accidentally broke others.

One of the best boba bars in the city was only two blocks away. Dad put his hazards on and waited by the curb as I popped in to order. When I climbed back into the car with a boba tea for each of us in my hands, the smooth sides of the cup in my hand shifted my energy. The hot stressful meeting in Dr. Kim's office was over. The anticipation of the sweet milky tea and chewy bubbles filled my awareness. I popped a straw through the plastic top. But as much as I wanted to move on, as I watched the tapioca beads travel through the straw I couldn't help but think of your eggs getting sucked up the barrel of a syringe.

REFLECTION QUESTIONS

- When a child is transitioning, the whole family experiences a transition. One of the big changes is revising our dreams about your family's future. The political climate and fear of the unknown can get parents caught in anxious rumination about the future. If you were to lean into Nelson Mandela's wish, "May your choices reflect your hopes not your fears," what choices and dreams would you consider for your family? Knowing that there are many ways to build a family, what are your dreams for your child's family life?

- What conversations have you had, or could you have with your child about creating a family for themselves when they grow up?
- Knowing that thinking about their own reproduction at the age of 12 or 13 or 14 is a significant developmental disruption for your child, how can you use your creative gifts to shape an age-appropriate conversation or series of conversations?
- What would it be like to look through family baby pictures together? What would it be like to talk about how involved or not involved your own parents were in your decision to become a parent? Could family holidays or rituals be a time to talk about generations and all the ways that new generations both change and continue family traditions?

Letter 17

December 2019: Taking Out the Trash

"What's wrong?" I asked. I could barely make out the words spilling from your mouth, something about mental illness? A mental disorder? You were sitting on your bed sobbing. It seemed the internet had coughed up something about being trans and mental disorders. This was the beginning of a new phase for you, a normal one in growing up, when kids need to kick the tires of their parents' belief systems. For many kids we knew, this meant developing their own political opinions or trying out new diets, but because gender diversity was controversial in the outside world, I knew it would be hard for you to grow into your own understanding of gender without interrogating whether Dad and I had made good on your behalf. It's one reason I've been writing these letters in the first place. I want you to have as honest an account as I can deliver—not to prove that Dad and I have been right, but so that you will have something concrete to point to, a record of the process that you can eventually judge for yourself. But before even handing you my notes, the internet and all its wild perspectives on gender was forcing you to ask the question of whom you could trust.

A part of me ached with the particular suffering mothers experience when their children suffer. I hated that you had to go through this. There were so many topics you were going to have to sort through for yourself, and I knew this was just the beginning. But another part of me had had it, not with you, but with the whole dilemma of whether being trans was a mental disorder. It is not. Just like being gay is not a mental disorder. But of course, if your condition appeared in the American Psychiatric Association's (APA) DSM, the handbook of mental disorders, you were going to wonder about what to believe. Who were you going to trust? Your mother or the diagnostic handbook and authority of the APA?

This was not the first time we'd had to consider the history of the DSM. Once I asked you if you thought you were transgender, and you paused for a minute, then said, "Mom, I just don't like that word. I don't know. I just don't like how it sounds." You were 11, and it was as if you could feel the heavy history that trailed behind the term even without knowing it. I wanted you to know that your discomfort put you in good company. Jack Halberstam, a gender-expansive writer, had written a whole book about "the powerful nature of naming—claiming a name or refusing to and thus remaining unnameable,"* and the dilemmas that the gender-diverse community faced with language and categorization. And the word "transgender" is one of a family of words that have been assigned to the community of gender-diverse people, often with a lot of associated stigma, which is one reason I did not doubt the word felt uncomfortable to you.

In the nineteen-twenties and thirties a German physician named Magnus Hirschfeld studied and treated patients whose

* Halberstam, Jack. *Trans*: A Quick and Quirky Account of Gender Variability.* University of California Press, 2018.

sexual orientation and gender identity did not conform to the norms of their times. Much of his legacy was destroyed in the Second World War by the Nazis. And the iconic book-burning images from that era are often images of Dr. Hirschfeld's research being burned. Dr. Harry Benjamin, who is credited with establishing the first standards of care for transgender patients (although the word he used was "transvestite"), had studied with Dr. Hirschfeld, and when Dr. Benjamin published his book about transgender care, he titled it The Transsexual Phenomenon.

In the nineteen-fifties, issues of gender identity were thought to be conflicts between individuals and their socially assigned role (rather than, say, with their endocrine system), and so were dealt with as psychiatric problems, which led to their inclusion in the DSM. First published in 1952 (we actually have a copy at home that I can show you; Dad found it for me online), the closest term to "transgender" to appear was "transvestitism," which was categorized as a sexual deviation, under the same topic heading that included homosexuality, pedophilia, and sexual sadism. All these diagnoses were considered personality disorders and sexual perversions. Enacting many of the behaviors in the category would have been illegal, which made it socially precarious to identify as gender nonconforming.

In 1973, the diagnosis for homosexuality was removed from the DSM, in a resolution written by the APA that claimed, "We will no longer insist on a label of sickness for individuals who insist that they are well and demonstrate no generalized impairment in social effectiveness."* But the diagnosis of transvestitism

* Lyons, R.D. (1973) "Psychiatrists, in a shift, declare homosexuality no mental illness." *The New York Times*, December 16. www.nytimes.com/1973/12/16/archives/psychiatrists-in-a-shift-declare-homosexuality-no-mental-illness.html

remained intact. In addition, two new diagnoses, "transsexualism" and "gender identity disorder," were introduced in 1980. Although these new diagnoses represented progress, they were still considered disorders. It was not until 2013 that gender identity disorder was replaced with the term "gender dysphoria." The introduction of the term was newsworthy because the experience of gender incongruence was no longer described as a disorder (despite appearing in a manual of mental disorders). American clinicians were making the point that being trans was not a psychological disorder that might need "curing." This was the kind of history that lurked in the shadows of the word transgender, and when I heard you say you didn't like it, I wanted you to know that feeling ambivalent about the word didn't have to mean feeling ambivalent about yourself.

When I found you crying in your room, though, I wasn't sure how to respond. I debated whether to lead from my empathetic side or challenge you to find your strength. It probably surprised you when I told you to hand over your iPad and get that internet trash out of your brain. I couldn't protect you from the cruelty or misunderstanding of others, but it felt important to express that ingesting that cruelty under my roof was not allowed. I was reminded of something I had heard Aimee Stephens say at a reception in Washington, *Don't let others tell you who you are.* You've always known who you are, and I want you to hold on to that confidence. You are the expert in your experience, and sometimes that will mean you'll need to reject outside information. As your mother, it's been my job to be the expert about your experience on your behalf, but it is also right for you to begin to demote me. The yardstick I've used to evaluate outside information over the years has been simple—did the information help you or harm you?

The season before you switched schools and started using the name Jake, I often found you hanging around the house wearing a furry light-blue mascot head. I'd be making dinner at the stove, then I'd turn around and across the kitchen, you'd be sitting at the table with that round, soft alpaca head on your shoulders. You wore it while you sat on the couch and watched TV. Sometimes you wore it in the car. I always laughed when you surprised me with that thing. But at night I would hear you crying in your bed. That fall, the darkening afternoons seemed to last a whole week. On the days you did not have rock climbing practice, you sat inside and drew manga characters and comic strips. On bad days, when I found you lying on your bed looking at the wall, I tried to get you out of the house to a park or to the water.

You were seeing a gender specialist we had been referred to by your endocrinologist. You initially balked at the idea of therapy, but I explained to you that you needed to be seen by someone for six months in order to obtain a letter of support so that your hormone blockers would be covered by insurance. You understood this was important because the blockers cost thousands of dollars a month. This was all the convincing you needed. But you complained every time you had to go. You told me the problem with the sessions was that they were boring. You told me I was paying a lot of money for you to play Monopoly with the therapist. About four months into your therapy, your complaining led me to ask her about her experience with gender-expansive kids like you. She paused for a minute, and then told me she had worked as a gender specialist with two other kids. We had already put in four months, and I didn't want to start the clock running again with someone new, so I continued to make you go. But she was the therapist we were stuck with when you seemed so low.

Palo Alto had a long history of poor mental health outcomes for kids. A 2016 study by the Centers for Disease Control and Prevention reported that teens in Palo Alto were four times more likely to kill themselves by suicide than the national average. The students who had considered suicide had a few traits in common: they had missed school in the previous month, they had experienced bullying, they had used drugs or alcohol in the past, or they identified as lesbian, gay, or bisexual. Being transgender was not mentioned. That said, a separate study by the CDC, entitled the Youth Risk Behavior Surveillance Study found that 47.7% of LGBTQ students, compared to 13.3% of heterosesual students had seriously considered suicide. The combination of living in Palo Alto and being LGBTQ put you at high risk.* For female-to-male teens it was even higher. In one study done by the American Academy of Pediatrics, over 50 percent of trans males aged 15–24 had tried to kill themselves.

I didn't want to take any chances with your low mood and consulted right away with your therapist. She was visibly concerned and suggested pulling you from school to see her three times a week. I resisted. Your problem was social. You had been cut off from sleepovers and playdates and birthday parties. School was the only place where you were able to see your friends. At lunchtime, you played wall ball or Connect Four. In the afternoon, you went to practice for the flag football team. You loved your history teacher. Taking time away from what was working felt like the wrong thing to do. But the therapist was adamant and told me the situation was very serious. I asked her if we could wait until winter break to do the multiple sessions a week, but she didn't

* https://afsp.org/suicide-statistics

think waiting was a good idea. We went back and forth about what to do. I was concerned for you, but I also worried that her plan would make things worse.

At one point, I stared across the office toward her desk and let my eyes ease their focus. In that brief fuzzy moment, my vision of your adult-self slipped into my awareness. It had only been a day or two before that, when I had been falling asleep, that I'd had the vision of you by my bedside holding the hand of the child for the very first time. Since that experience, even though I was worried, I had carried the feeling of your wholeness within me. The stakes were as high as they had ever been, but a part of me had confidence that you would be okay, that you were okay. The rest of me was terrified.

I was afraid to reject the advice of a paid professional, and plus, we were close to fulfilling the six-month gender therapy requirement for your letter of support. I asked her again if we could do the multiple appointments after school let out for break, and she said, "It's your call. You are the parent," in a way that made it clear she would not have made the same call herself.

While stopped at a red light on the way home from her office I started to sob. My wails filled the car. The fear of not knowing whether I was making the right call, and the possibility that you might become another tragic Palo Alto story, wracked my whole body. But when the light turned green, I had to drive. I dragged my sleeve across my face. By muscle memory I gripped myself together as I had many times before. I filed the therapist's doubt in my judgment into a sealed vault of thoughts I would not allow myself to have.

The weekend following that appointment you were low. And rather than let your mood stagnate in the house, I took you to a local marina. Small boats bobbed in the bay. A chipped gray dock limped out over the water, and a rusty embankment held the land from crumbling. We threw a frisbee to keep busy.

You asked me a question between throws.

"Mom, do you think there is a heaven?" The question scared me. With your sad mood and with everything I knew about the statistics, I could not help but feel queasy wondering if you were thinking about dying.

"Well, I don't think it's that simple. But I think our souls will be okay. Like I think they keep going after our bodies are gone."

"Yeah, I think God had me born a girl for a reason. I think there's a reason for it," you said before you tossed me the frisbee one more time. I understood then that you envisioned yourself becoming a man in the future. You had never insisted on being a boy before, but by that fall you had traveled far enough away from girl that, this one afternoon, when you said that you were born a girl for a reason, it felt complete, as if girlhood was already in the past, which I had to agree, it was. The unspoken part of the conversation that afternoon was what you did not say about how afraid you were of growing up trans. I feared you were weighing up whether or not it would be worth the effort. But I also sensed that the pleasure of throwing the disc back and forth, with the salty smell of the water around us, comforted you. You were facing a terrifying process, but in the sense that God had a plan for you, I knew you had come up with a mindset of hope.

As you handed me your iPad in your bedroom the other night, I hoped I had done alright. And maybe especially if I hadn't, I hoped I had modeled the confidence you would need to toss off the burden of wrongheaded adults, even if it eventually turns out that I have been one of them.

REFLECTION QUESTIONS

- Research shows that having one supportive parent significantly improves the mental health outcomes for transgender youth. What experiences in your family's gender journey supports this research? How has supporting your child's mental health activated your values? How has their mental health challenged you?
- Do you feel you have identified the supports your child needs? If not, what organization or individual might help you find more resources?
- As a parent it is natural to want our children's lives to be happy and conflict-free, and we also know that challenge builds character. How do you see your child's resilience and strength growing while they navigate their gender journey?

Interview
Andrew Hedges on Internalized Transphobia and the Fight for Identity

Andrew Hedges is a manager at the Women's Research Center and LGBTQ+ Student Center at the University of Central Oklahoma. He is also a member of the Army National Guard who transitioned during the Trump administration.

Cristina: Andrew, talk to me a little bit about your story and how you ended up in the military.

Andrew: It wasn't until my sophomore year in high school that I understood something wasn't lining up. For some time, I had personally identified as gay. But everybody was like, you're a lesbian. It was my lesbian identity that started the rift within my family as well as within my friend group. It was complicated. Who could come over? Who could I hang out with? What type of people were okay? And that led me to see Stephen Black who is a conversion therapist in Oklahoma. I first saw him when I was 13 years old. My dad lied to me about where we were going, and then it just was like, we're here. And I turned to my dad and said, this isn't mom's office.

Cristina: I'm really sorry that happened to you.

Andrew: I always say that conversion therapy did work. It turned me into a boy and I'm straight now! A terrible joke. But I think it's funny.

In junior year one of my friends was identifying as nonbinary. I didn't know what that was. And I didn't know I could do that. So I started researching, but I had to do it very secretly, because my dad was an IT guy. I couldn't do anything on the computer at home or anything on my phone, because it all would have been traced. So I did all this at friends' houses. I was at a school library on the computer trying to figure out if a girl can be a guy. I had always heard of men transitioning to women in movies, terrible portrayals, of course. So I thought, well, if that can happen then sure, it can go the other way, right? And finally, after researching and researching, I figured out that yes, this is something you can do. But it's not something you can do right now. So, you just push it down in there, and let it fester, like a powder keg.

After my senior year of high school, I went to New Mexico to work at a Boy Scout camp called Philmont. The day before I left, I cut off all my hair. I had, hair down to here, and I just lobbed it off. When my mom saw me the day before I left she was very displeased. I went off to summer camp and was a counselor and a gunslinger and was able to live in the Wild West, which was a blast. And during that time, I met people from other states such as Chicago, New York, and California—people whose minds were a lot more open than mine was at the time. I also started reading a lot of books and one of them was *Some Assembly Required* by Arin Andrews, which I think every parent should read.

I realized Arin Andrews was from Tulsa, Oklahoma, and that

I had to talk to him, but was sure he was not going to want to talk to me. Then I found out he was going to the same college I was going to in the fall. I messaged him on Instagram, and said, "Hey, I'm thinking about transitioning, I just read your book, and we're both starting at OSU. Can I talk to you one day?" And he got back to me. We met outside the student union and talked for a while and had lunch together. I was kind of like, okay, I think this is what, you know, I want to get into, but I have to wait until I can figure something out insurance wise. I was already on track to join the army. I wanted to be in it since I was a little kid. And I already auditioned for the band, because you have to audition before you can even go to the processing stuff for the army. I didn't talk to anybody or anyone about any gender problems I was having at the moment, because I knew that that wasn't gonna fly. I knew that "Don't ask, don't tell" was still in effect even though it was supposed to be gone. And so I went to boot camp at Fort Jackson, South Carolina, that winter. Before I left for boot camp I had written my family a letter explaining my gender to them, and the day they got it they drove straight to campus to meet me. They pulled out this funny almanac of papers, all these reasons they had found why people shouldn't transition. I was hoping for some support to figure stuff out, but instead I got all this resistance and negativity.

I'll never forget after I graduated from boot camp my mom and I were talking on the phone one night and she said, "Did the army kind of like, kick that out of you?" And I replied, "What do you mean?" So, she says, "You know did the army fix you?" And I was like, "Oh, did going to boot camp make me more of a woman? Um no, sorry. It didn't make it worse, but also it didn't 'fix it.'"

I ended up growing really close to my sergeants, and I felt like

I could eventually tell them what was up. I told them I identified as trans, and I was trying to figure out what I could do. One reason I joined was so that I could have health insurance and a little bit of money to live off of, because I knew the moment I would get back home I wouldn't be able to be there anymore. The sergeants told me that they would print off everything they could and give it to me, but that's really all they were able to do, because they didn't know anything about it. So, I received a little manila envelope with the Obama-era guidance. It was 2016. Trump just had been elected, and his whole thing banning trans people wasn't out until January 2017. I began a long, contentious process of trying to get my identity affirmed by the Army. I ended up just going ahead and starting testosterone. The hilarious thing was that my insurance covered it. Yep. The military, because men get testosterone all the time. And so, a vial for testosterone was 15 bucks on Tricare for me, great. It was nothing. And I was like, this is fantastic. Let's, you know, just keep it up. Eventually, my voice kind of started getting lower, facial hair took a while still, as you know, but you know, we succumb. And so, I remember one of the guys who sat next to me in our band, and he was like, you know, are you feeling alright? Your voice like, seems really loud. I was like, oh, yeah. I'm just a little sick, you know, it's just allergies, or whatever, and kind of played out off his idea. Then I was like, okay, well, now, now we're gonna have to figure something out.

My goal was to get my name changed and my gender marker changed on the civilian side and on the military side. When we got a new commander, he was like, alright, what you need to do is get everything changed on the civilian side. So I went and did all that. I got my passport changed and everything. And so federally, hey, I'm a male. My passport says it, my license says it,

Social Security knows—all this stuff says male. And then when I brought it all back to the Army, they were like, yep, no, we're still not going to recognize this. So, I was like, okay, well why is this still not working? And they're like, you need to have both, you need to have all your surgeries. And I said, okay, what are all my surgeries? Tell me. What are they? And they were like, well, you have to remove your breasts. And you have figure out what you're going to do for your bottom surgery, basically. I said, okay, well, I've been wanting to get top surgery for like, the past four years. But you all have told me no. So since that's good, let me go call the doctor, I'll go get that scheduled. And so I did. And I went and got surgery, and all of that. And then it was this past summer, I had surgery. And it's hilarious, because go to Fort Carson, Colorado over the summer with my unit, and my name is changed and all that stuff. Even on my government travel card, it has my new name on it, which is great. It's fantastic. But they wrote me up with a female gender marker after top surgery after being on testosterone for like, four years now...

Cristina: After every hoop they asked you to jump through?

Andrew: It's because I haven't had bottom surgery yet. That was the reason. So thankfully, I bunked with one of my really good friends. And I thought, how weird is this? It's crazy, because a lot of people don't have bottom surgery.

Here is where a lot of discrepancy lies. And where I think a lot of it has to do with where we're at state wise. I don't know if you saw that Oklahoma's governor got all in hoops about one person in our state changing their gender to "X" for nonbinary. It just blew up. It was all over the place in our local news. Even under the

Obama guidelines things did not go correctly. And I just couldn't make it work. I did enjoy times that I had in the military. And I would have continued if things were fixed. But the belief systems that everybody had, especially, like, on the medical side, and was like nope, there is only one way to do this, which is obviously not true. I just couldn't keep trying to push everything through. There's a group called Sparta. They are a trans advocacy group for people who are in the military who have retired and are veterans. And so, I even contacted them and got in with, like, jag lawyers and everything like that. And they were like, everything they're doing is wrong. This isn't right. We're gonna call them. And they did. And still nothing ever happened. So, I got to the point where I just realized nothing's going to change. I was passed up on a promotion. They passed me up because of my transition packet. And because that was still floating around, and nobody was going to pick it up. At that point I was, like, I don't want to be a part of this organization anymore.

Cristina: Wow, that was so challenging. So disappointing and intense. I'm sorry you had to deal with that. What do you think it has to say more generally about living a trans life? And what would you want parents to know?

Andrew: The experience was definitely challenging. And it was wrong to have to go through it. But if you asked me where my own resilience comes from, I would say it comes from seeing how far I've come. Why would I give up now? I've already gotten this far, not just transition wise. I mean, that's even school wise, you know, I could have been a drop out, but now I'm in graduate school.

For parents I would say, give kids space to breathe and grow on their own. You don't always have to be a safety net. You don't always have to be the helicopter parent who is always there to catch kids when they fall. Because sometimes we do have to fall in order to get back up and dust ourselves off and keep moving.

Letter 18

January 2020: Firsthand Experiences

The week after we met with Dr. Kim, she called to confirm that my understanding of my college classmate's story was correct. Her son had, indeed, retrieved oocytes without having discontinued his blockers. It was amazing news. We had two experimental procedures to choose from, surgical extraction of either an ovary or ovarian tissue, or a cycle of egg retrieval that would follow a relatively conventional regimen of follicle-stimulating hormone injections. Still, both options were intimidating. They were intrusive and experimental and had associated risks. Tissue extraction included the typical risks associated with surgeries and general anesthesia. Follicle stimulation, especially an experimental version of it, risked ovarian hyperstimulation syndrome, a reaction to high doses of the hormones used to make follicles grow, which led to pain and nausea and in very rare cases, death. I'm still in shock about it. After months of working to generate options, we did it. Dr. Kim's news arrived just in time—just three months before you turn 14 and start "T."

The same week we heard from Dr. Kim, I had the opportunity to have dinner with S. Bear Bergman, a trans author whose work I admire. One of his essays appeared in a book called *Gender*

Outlaws, and he had published an essay collection of his own entitled *The Nearest Exit May Be Behind You*. His description of gender dysphoria struck me as the most similar to the experience I saw you having, so when I got the chance to organize a dinner with him, I jumped on it. A few other mothers of trans kids joined us at a restaurant near our house.

I recognized Bear as soon as he walked into the room. He wore a gray suit vest over a plaid flannel button-down. His eyes crinkled into a smile when he saw me. We shook hands, sat down at the table, and chatted while we waited for the others. When my friends arrived, we ordered a round of drinks. Champagne for the mothers, ginger ale for Bear. Throughout the evening, he stroked his beard with his right hand, and I spent the night thinking on and off about your creamy cheeks, imagining the beard you might grow after you start testosterone. You had always said you wanted a soul patch. I could almost see it in my mind, but I still couldn't wrap my head around the idea of your buttery skin turning to sandpaper. I imagine lots of boy moms feel this way.

When I told Bear that I had been to the Supreme Court to hear the oral arguments for *Harris v. Stephens*, he said, "I am not sorry I moved to Toronto. Let's just say that," then shook his head in a way that implied the USA had tired him out. I shared with the group that David Cole, Aimee Stephens' lead counsel, had visited our home briefly. He told us he thought he was going to lose the case, but then said optimistically, "Look, this is just the beginning, it will probably take another 15 years or so, but we'll get there." I didn't have to explain to this group that his comment had utterly failed to comfort me. We looked at each other grimly and changed the subject.

Over the course of dinner, everyone talked about their kids, including Bear. We told your ages and described how each of you experienced your emerging gender. When it was my turn, I told Bear about our trip to see Dr. Kim and how unsettled it made me feel that I had heard about the possibility of preserving your fertility without going off blockers before she did. I explained that between the Supreme Court case, the trip to the reproductive endocrinologist, and the ongoing news headlines from the Trump administration, the world felt more chaotic by the day. And I felt more afraid.

"Your experience sounds very typical, if you don't mind me saying," he said, smiling.

> You're part of the tradition now. Information in the trans community has always passed faster through networks of people than it has through institutions. And trans people have always had to help each other to negotiate for the care they have needed. Like in the sixties and seventies, when the Johns Hopkins clinic, which was far from perfect in so many ways, was doing the first transition surgeries, there was this eighty-page questionnaire that trans women had to fill out to be approved for the surgery. Imagine a survey based on the fantasies these white-cis-guy-doctors had about the perfect woman—imagine filling in the blanks on that thing. Well, practically no one could pass the test. But once one person did—then everyone did. That is how our community has gotten by. We hand each other along to get what we need.

I had never thought of it that way; the experts had never been the experts on the trans experience. The real wisdom had always come and probably always would come from the real-life experiences of trans people. The way I had acquired information about your fertility was not random at all; it was the way knowledge moved in this community. Like digital packets on the web, discrete bits of information spread from person to person across the network. The data darted in small bits across many paths at once. This felt familiar to me in a way. Speed, on-demand delivery, chaotic redundancy. This was what made the internet so fast and robust. If one network path was blocked, there was always another one available. As a trans person, or the parent of a trans person, being part of a community mattered more than having the "right" information. Because in reality, there was no "right" information. It was all changing so fast.

I exhaled. The bubbles of my champagne glass glittered like sequins in the candle light. I looked around the table at Bear and the other moms. One of the moms was an old friend I had known for years before either of us knew we had trans kids. And the other woman was a new friend, a writer who had always been a ghost writer, but now she was writing in her own voice for the first time. I loved these women. We were bound together in a sisterhood that was new but already felt as reliable and comfortable as a favorite pair of jeans. Bear smiled. "I'm tired of the gloom and doom," he said. "Yeah, the world is broken. There is no shortage of stuff to scream about. And yet, look, here we are." Then we all clinked glasses.

REFLECTION QUESTIONS

- Think of a future in which gender diversity is celebrated and you feel your child is completely safe to be themselves. What are your dreams for your child? What dreams would you want them to be able to consider?

- What would it be like for the USA to elect its first trans president?
- What about a future in which trans folx were valued for their unique perspective and sought after as editors, movie producers, school administrators, or generals in charge of a gender-diverse climate protection brigade?
- What if your child's gender is not a hindrance, but is one of their greatest assets? How does the future look then? And how would it change your parenting if you considered your child's gender as a rare version of giftedness?

Letter 19

January 2020: Building Community

I flew to Oklahoma because of the wish I made at the Supreme Court to connect with a nationwide person-to-person network of LGBTQ+ friendly people. Oklahoma was a state I had never visited and was one of over 20 states that didn't have laws prohibiting gender identity discrimination. It was part of a territory that sometimes triggered a bit of coastal prejudice in me. The idea of you someday visiting a place like Oklahoma made me feel nervous, and I thought the best cure was to get the real facts about the place by getting my feet on the ground there.

On Transgender Day of Remembrance last November, I donated money to Free Mom Hugs, an organization of LGBTQ+ supportive moms who attended Pride Parades. In the past, I had supported other LGBTQ+ organizations, but that fall I felt frustrated that I didn't know my fellow citizens better and was exhausted by how intimidated Trump and his Make America Great Again followers were making me feel about your future. I wanted to believe that our country was more than red states and blue states, and as scared as I was, I imagined that families raising trans or gay kids in red states were feeling even more vulnerable than we were.

Everything I knew about the organization came from its website. I liked that its founder, Sara Cunningham, characterized herself as Christian woman with a gay kid, who was saying, "Enough is enough." I saw her as being on the front lines of the cultural battle for LGBTQ+ acceptance. Life for trans kids would be slow to change in Sara's community, and communities like hers, even if the Supreme Court decided in favor of Aimee Stephens.

My phone rang shortly after I made my donation; I assumed there was some kind of problem with the transaction and answered. The voice on the other end of the line sounded like honey, rich and lustrous, and inexplicably warm. It was Sara. She was calling to say thank you and hello. I've made charitable donations in the past, but I've never had the founder of the organization call me directly. It turned out I had been the first person to use their new online donation button, and they were so excited about it that Sara had picked up the phone to call me herself.

Her impulse to reach out astonished me, and I felt briefly young again as we re-enacted the ritual of a person-to-person phone call. I remembered the old beige phone in Nonny's house, with its coiled cord, and felt the same pleasant pop of surprise that always rose in the back of my head when I received an unexpected call from a friend. That this way of connecting had become old fashioned suddenly struck me as sad.

Sweetheart, this is important. We live in a part of the country that prides itself in its ability to innovate. Whether we like Mark Zuckerberg or not, his famous quote, "Move fast and break things," is as apt a tagline as any for where we live. Speed drives our culture. Scale up. Launch first. Grab market share. Disrupt. Our family has loved and benefited from the drive and creativity and possibility that accompanies these precepts. But these values also cast long shadows. One of them is the way our collective ambition dehumanizes our connections. I'm embarrassed, and should be, that getting on the phone for a call can register to me as a drain on my time. Jake, a person-to-person real-time phone call is an essential connection. No system or circuit board, no government or company, or AI, runs on the engine of mutual care. Humans do. This is a feature, not a bug, even though the speed of technology might try to persuade us otherwise. Scale, one of our Silicon Valley mantras, dilutes human connection.

I don't recall if Sara and I made our plan on that call or on a subsequent one; all I know is that once the sound of her voice was in my ear, I wanted to meet her. It was as if its timbre carried both the loss and the light of her family's experience. Sara's conservative Christian church had been the heart and soul of her life before her son Parker told her he was gay. After he came out, Sara's community forced her to choose between the faith life she knew and her relationship with her son. Her loyalty to her son had catapulted her into isolation and a redefined relationship with God. Founding Free Mom Hugs became her way to build the community she wished her family had had during the lonely years they spent rebuilding their lives. I booked my trip to Oklahoma City because I wanted to be part of her community too.

When Sara greeted me outside the doors of baggage claim in Oklahoma City, she walked straight up to me, cupped her palms around my face, and looked into my eyes. "You are even more beautiful in person. I love you," she said. I had never had a stranger look at me straight in the eyes with that kind of intensity. Her gaze penetrated my core. I felt naked from the inside out, as if her soul was looking at interior parts of me that had never been seen before. I couldn't imagine anyone else doing this without frightening or overpowering me. But with Sara, it was as if she poured her warmth directly into the cup of my heart where it radiated out all the way to my fingertips and toes. I was about to learn that this was Sara's superpower, a preternatural ability to connect with people on a soul level.

We drove to her house in her jeep. The cover for the spare tire, which hung on the back, was adorned with the Free Mom Hugs rainbow logo. Her home was a modest two-story colonial in a neighborhood in which all the streets were arranged in a perfect grid. It was winter, and the trees on her property had lost their leaves. I got the sense that her house was especially lively in summer. There was an above-ground pool in the backyard and next to it a sheltered outdoor patio decorated with party lights. I could imagine them twinkling on hot summer nights.

Inside, I met Parker, her son, and dropped off my bags in her guest room. I offered her a bag of tangerines I had picked off our trees, and we spent some time visiting in the family room, where Ruthie, her little Chihuahua-Dachshund mix, climbed up onto my lap. Later, we went out for dinner with a few other members of the Free Mom Hugs team at a restaurant in a funky neighborhood called the Plaza, where the buildings were painted with colorful murals and stores sold folk art, vintage clothing, and locally crafted jewelry. The restaurant served southern food, craft beers, and hand-stirred cocktails. I ordered a spicy margarita and ribs. During dinner, a group of strangers from the other side of the restaurant stopped by our table. "Are you that mom who gives out hugs?" they asked. And the next thing I knew, everyone was hugging everyone, and Sara was saying in her honey voice, "Now you take care of yourself, okay?"

Over the next few days, Sara toured me around her home city.

Everywhere we stopped, she met someone she knew, or someone she didn't know approached her for a hug. There were always hugs. We drove through many neighborhoods of Oklahoma City. Neighborhoods with brick mansions and manicured lawns and others like hers, drawn in a cozy grid of streets, with old frontier-style bungalows painted in every color. The commercial center of the city was dominated by Devon Tower, a 50-story modern skyscraper completed in 2012 that served as the local headquarters for Devon Energy. There were a few city corners that reminded me of some of the grittier sections of San Francisco, although far smaller. Like San Francisco, the air on these blocks was laced with pot smoke.

Sara's first stop for me was the Diversity Center of Oklahoma, where I met Kelley Blair, the director. Kelley is a member of a Native American tribe and identifies as Two-Spirit. They run a multidisciplinary gender clinic for the city's trans population. With a lobby and only a few small offices, it offers sophisticated care. Kelley, who is a social worker, has designed a care program grounded in the philosophy of the medicine wheel, in which every person's health is evaluated based on four quadrants—physical health, mental health, spiritual health, and community health. Through the medicine wheel she addresses a broader sense of wellbeing than any gender specialist we've ever met in the Bay Area. Having visited almost too many specialists to count, I realized that not a single provider had ever asked us about your spiritual life or your community life, even though the research about trans lives indicates so strongly that social support is critical to trans wellbeing. Occasionally I'd been asked if you struggled with your peers or if you experienced bullying, but no one had asked about your community overall, and certainly no one had thought to bring up your spiritual life, even though you, yourself, had brought it up to me when you asked me if I thought God had made you born a girl for a reason. Visiting the Diversity Center and meeting Kelley reminded me that a purely scientific approach to a topic as complex as gender would never capture the emotional and social complexity of gender diversity. It was eye-opening to realize there were novel resources for you in Oklahoma.

Later that day, Sara took me to a shelter in the basement of a church that housed homeless youth, some of whom were trans. I was there the night the community was celebrating someone's successful completion of her GED exam. A group stood at the end of a set of bunk beds and crowded around their friend, who was showing them her certificate of completion. It was a celebration scene with laughter and congratulations and huge smiles. In another room around the corner, a smaller group of three or four kids were squeezed onto a couch, watching television. Altogether there were about a dozen kids staying there, and my understanding was that since the weather had become cold, all the beds were full, and some nights they turned kids away. The circumstances were unarguably harsh, grim even, but there was an element of light that I was starting to recognize from other experiences I had had visiting other pockets of the LGBTQ+ community.

The morning I was leaving Oklahoma, a news headline dropped. The South Dakota legislature was proposing a new state law that would make it illegal for doctors to prescribe hormone blockers to minors. It was the first time, as far as I knew, that such a law was being proposed. The law targeted the very drugs you had been taking for over a year and a half, the medicine that paused your endogenous puberty. Making them illegal would essentially mean that no trans youth living in South Dakota would have access to the medicines available to help bring their gender into alignment before adulthood, forcing many to live with debilitating and potentially life-threatening cases of gender dysphoria. It was hard for me to believe a law like this could even be proposed. And while this bill didn't impact you directly, there was always the threat that it would generate a lawsuit that might make it to the Supreme Court. Given the discourse I had heard while there, this possibility terrified me.

When I got home, I called Sara right away and asked her to put me in touch with the Free Mom Hugs chapter leader in South Dakota. And you know what I did? I called that mom right away. I told her I lived in California, and I cared, and I wanted to support her during this scary time. Not that she needed my help. The Free Mom Hugs chapter lead in South Dakota, Susan Ann, was a formidable activist. She had already mobilized her community and was actively collaborating with the ACLU to block the progression of the bill. What mattered most to her right then was that someone who didn't know her had called and told her that we cared about her work. We understood that what happened in South Dakota mattered to the families of trans kids across the country. I was able to help her out by participating in a video talking about why affirmative care mattered and rallying our community in California to email the South Dakota governor. By February, the bill had failed in the state senate, and Kristi Noem, the Republican South Dakota governor, reported that she rarely received as many emails about a state bill as she did around the one we helped block.

Interview

Dr. Nick Teich on the Importance of Community and Chosen Family

Nick Teich founded Camp Aranu'tiq in 2009. It's one of the first overnight camps in the USA to serve gender-diverse youth. Nick has over a dozen years' experience running camps. He works year-round on all facets of Harbor Camps.* He holds a PhD in Social Policy from Brandeis University and a Master's degree in Social Work from Boston College.

Cristina: Would you tell us a little bit about your story, and how you decided to start a camp for gender-diverse kids?

Nick: Sure. As a kid I went to overnight camp in Maine for eight weeks, every summer, starting when I was ten. It was a girl's camp. I didn't know I was trans at the time. But I cut my hair short, I looked like a boy, well, sort of, and I was accepted for who I was at camp. And it was the one place I always wanted to be during any season. I have lifelong friends from that camp who I'm still very close to today. As I got older—I transitioned in my early

* https://harborcamps.org

twenties, right after college—I started to think about camp in the context of what would kids who know they're trans or nonbinary, or gender-variant, as we were really saying at that time, what would they do about overnight camp? Because overnight camp is such a wonderful resource for kids, and how would that go? And around the same time, I was volunteering at a charity camp that was one-week long, because I couldn't live without camp.

And when I came out to the board of directors who billed themselves as liberal and open-minded, their original response was supportive, and they told me: that's great. This was 2007, kind of 200 years ago in trans years. Ultimately, they decided that I would not be allowed back for, "the good of the kids." It was a moment that really struck me because I didn't expect it. I had been privileged to not face a lot of discrimination. And that's when I really started thinking deeply about camp in the context of trans kids.

Cristina: I'm really sorry that you've had to go through that.

Nick: Well, I think that moment led to the beginning of Camp Aranu'tiq and Harbor Camps. That's how I'm able to look at it now. But it was very painful at the time. Camp Aranu'tiq started as a one week-long session with 42 campers in our first year. We were able to rent a camp in Connecticut at the end of their season. And it went great. The rest is history. It expanded exponentially in New Hampshire. This upcoming summer, we will serve a little over 400 campers in the regular overnight, and then another 350 in our family camps.

Cristina: That's amazing. Your camp has been a tremendously positive experience for our family. We're just so lucky for the journey that you've been on with camp. I think it's provided so much, to so many. Which leads me to my next question. Can you talk to me about why community is so important to gender-diverse kids? What does it provide? And can you speak a little bit about "chosen family," maybe even what that term means to you, and how you think camp may be a part of that?

Nick: Community is the biggest part of it for us. And that's exactly what the camp is for. I mean, our mission is confidence, resilience, and community building in trans and nonbinary youth. If you came to camp and just sat down, right where you arrived, and didn't move for one, two, or three weeks, you'd still get community. And that's huge. I can't overstate just how important it is to have other people who understand you and understand your journey. People who know what it's like to go through things that you've gone through, and there's so many differences; you can't be with another trans person and assume that they've gone through everything you've gone through, but there's a relaxation that happens when you're around other people who are like you. It's feeling like I don't have to be on guard, like I can relax and be myself. And that's the biggest thing that we want—for kids to be able to do just that. Camp provides a place where they don't have to talk about it if they don't want to. We don't have formal groups or therapy groups or anything purposely because we want kids to just come to camp and be kids, and organically talk and connect about their experiences as much or as little as they want, knowing that they can walk into any bathroom, they can wear whatever they want, they can swim in whatever they want. And there's not going to be any issue or anybody looking at them in a strange way.

Cristina: Swimming especially is so great!

Nick: We've had campers who the reason that they didn't know how to swim in their teenage years was because they didn't know what bathing suit to put on. Or they didn't want to put on the bathing suit that they were "supposed to wear." So, it's amazing to see what can happen when you have kids who say I don't want to swim, and then when you tell them that everyone around you is trans or nonbinary, and everyone wears whatever they want. It changes things a lot. Having chosen family is along the same lines. It means having people who understand you and love you for who you are. Unfortunately, a lot of people's given family is not going to offer that unconditional support, whether they only support them on the surface or they don't support them at all. Or even ones that do support them. Kids in particular, but really everyone, needs to have friends and people that they can be themselves with unapologetically, and sometimes those are the people that end up becoming their chosen family. And those people are so much more meaningful in some cases than their actual family, if their actual family is not supportive.

Cristina: I'm curious, what advice or wishes would you have for parents of gender-diverse youth, about helping their kids to find or build community?

Nick: I would say it is important to find resources, if possible, in your area, that can get these kids together with other kids. The internet is not a substitute for that. It's a great place for these kids to find information that I could never find. As a kid, for instance, I didn't even know trans men existed until I met one, way later. But getting them in person with other trans people, or other nonbinary people, and letting them just be kids together and allowing those friendships to form is essential. If you're in an area where there's not that resource readily available—that's one of the reasons our camp exists. Getting that face-to-face interaction and being in person and having the ability to have a playdate or a sleepover, or hang out or see a movie, when we can do that again, is really important. Because that's how relationships work.

Letter 20

February 2020: Embodied Experience

The day of your sparring contest the taekwondo studio was packed. You had been going to the studio to learn your forms for years. At home, I loved watching you repeat your kicks or sashay down our hallways in a form when you thought I wasn't looking. For a child who sometimes had trouble focusing, there were two activities that never failed to engage you. One was drawing. We had stacks of black spiral notebooks full of your manga-style characters. The other activity was taekwondo. The two seemed related to me, the way they helped you integrate yourself and work with your body. In your artwork, you often drew male figures in various dramatic positions, sometimes penning sequences that told heroic stories. Your drawings of individual figures often depicted creative tension between two different energies. An astronaut holding a kitten, a rugged-faced fighter with a bone exposed, a deep-sea diver caring for an octopus. These practices gave you ways to integrate the competing energies in your own body.

We had signed you up for taekwondo as a kind of graduation from working with your occupational therapist, Leslie, after you no longer needed such specific sensory therapy. She had suggested it to us as a natural extension of the work you had done with her.

Your studio started all its sessions with meditation and a recitation of the team mantra before physical practice began. Over the years, you had progressed from white belt, and the winter of the sparring competition, you were about to graduate from blue belt to brown.

Sparring was not an important part of the culture in your studio. You had never done it, and to my knowledge, none of the other students had either. I had come to think of your practice sessions as a kind of yoga class, full of focus and strength building, but since the athleticism was emphasized so much more than fighting or self-defense, I had almost forgotten you were studying an ancient art of combat. Or that other people who studied taekwondo actually fought each other. That night your studio, usually airy and full of light, was stuffy and crowded. Students of all levels had come to participate, and all the teachers and assistants were on site with whistles to referee matches. The shriek of whistles and the smacks and grunts of fighting filled the air.

I assumed that you would be nervous, but your body was loose and limber. You laughed and smiled with your classmates. When you entered the ring to take on your first opponent, your shoulders lay relaxed along your back. But once the whistle blew, your feet shuffled back and forth across the competition space so fast I could hardly follow them. Your kicks and punches snapped across the circle. It took you less than ten minutes to win all the points in the match. I had not known what to expect from the matches, but I realized what was more profound was that I had not known what to expect from you. In the ring, you were calm, quick, strategic, focused. And strong.

The last person you bested that night was twice your size. He was nearly six feet tall and looked about three years older than you. Unfortunately for him, you were twice as fast. You beat him handily. The second night's session went much the same as the first. And you had come in first place. I was so disappointed that I had not been able to be there, but I loved receiving you at home as a champion. Your cheeks were pink, and your hair was sweaty. Light was shining from your eyes. I hugged you hard and then listened to you describe your matches while you ate a sundae with caramel sauce and hot fudge.

I thought back to the years that you saw Leslie and how much more grounded your body seemed to me now. Your walking and bike riding, your transitions in and out of the car or up and down stairs were all smoother. Your temper—yes, you still had one—seemed like it had retreated. When you were little, it felt like anger and frustration lived on your skin; the smallest disturbance woke them up. But over the years they seemed to live more peacefully inside of you. It felt like a sufficient buffer between the world and your body had finally been established. You were able to contain your anger and use it more productively; or if that wasn't possible, you knew how to take a break. It was hard for me to know exactly what external circumstances and internal changes had come together to produce your ability to regulate. Was it the mental and physical practice of taekwondo? Was it a simple fact of your growing maturity? Was it that you were living not only as a boy-ish person but as an actual boy?

During the Leslie years, when I was grappling with how to handle your dysregulation, I had turned to memoirs by trans writers to learn more about gender diversity. I was desperate for stories that were composed of the raw language of experience, descriptions from real people minus the doctors' translations. I read as many as I could find, as fast as I could. Different trans voices began to weave and overlap. I heard repeating patterns. As a group, the chorus of voices created something like a unified melody in my head. I had read nearly a dozen books by trans writers when I attended a writing conference that hosted a panel for trans writers. Each of the writers had prepared a talk for the session. They each had printed out their essay and then cut it into strips. At the panel session they combined all their paper strips into a cardboard box so that the essays recombined with one another. Then each writer took a turn reading from the box.

Their performance borrowed a form called cutups that a beat poet named William S. Burroughs had made famous. Burroughs had once said, "Perhaps when you cut into the present the future leaks out." And this was how it felt to me when I listened to those trans writers as they spontaneously created their montage of meaning. I teared up, because everyone's voices together amplified the narrative. The talk didn't have a traditional plot or flow. It didn't proceed in a straight line, but it was saturated with significance and emotional texture.

Watching you spar felt like a similar live recombination of meaning. Your arm, which had once flailed wildly, now sliced across space on your command. Your feet, which had previously crossed this way and that way and caused you to stumble, now danced backward and forward with precision. Your torso, which you previously seemed to hide behind a curled spine, was upright. Your muscles were strong, and the power from your core energized your moves and propelled you toward your opponent. You had claimed authority over your body, and you knew how to apply it.

The problem I had always had with the gender dysphoria diagnosis was how heavily it relied on stereotypes and on descriptions of superficial preferences. This had never aligned with what I saw in you as a child, or even how I experienced gender in my own childhood. What had been described in the diagnosis as a preference for rough-and-tumble play, for example, appeared in you as something more like a drive with the accompanying compulsion and lack of choice. I had vivid memories from my own childhood that carried the same intensity. A cardboard box full of Mardi Gras beads. Purple and gold and green. The way I shoved my hands in the slippery beads and grabbed them by the fistful. In another memory I remembered the sensation of swimming in the swimming pool behind my childhood home. I spent what seemed like an entire summer turning somersaults underwater one, two, three, four, five...up to eleven, and then twelve, and days later hit my record, thirteen. I craved the dizzy, weightless sensation of looping my body in the water.

Someone observing me could have called my interest in these sensations preferences, but I think they were more than that. I thought your sensory seeking was more than preferential too. The trans memoirs I read seemed to say the same thing to me. Each story felt like a facet of the larger whole. As an experiment, I collected sentences I found in trans memoirs that were imbued with similar energy. Some clustered around dysregulation and restlessness. Others hewed to the topic of shame and emotional confusion. One collection expressed the embodied experience of gender alignment. This collection came to mind when I watched you spar.

> I didn't expect the visceral pleasure. The unbridled freedom. This internal pull like a North-seeking compass. I know I am making the right decision because whenever I think about changing my gender I am flooded with feelings of relief. In movement I could feel myself in my body. Biking, rollerblading, running, climbing trees. I was a

digging machine, a stick winger. I was all of a piece proportioned once again. My rising pecs, the hard center of my abs. Something calm at the core of me, solid, cool and placid as a lake. What my body was good for.*

Once you had told me that you thought you would feel more at home in a boy's body, and I believed you. Watching you spar, I knew you were making that body your home. The longing for

* This small mosaic of text was inspired by a live panel discussion I attended at the annual conference for the Association of Writers & Writers Programs (commonly referred to as AWP) in 2019. The panel was called, "Transmorgification of the Transgender Narrative: Cunting up Trans Nonfiction." This panel, and the language that streamed from it, beamed out of it, influenced me profoundly. it elevated my understanding of my son's corporeal experience. Intellectually, I had the instant sense that I was bearing witness to human evolution and a collective struggle to language an experience that up until very recently went unnamed. I offer a deep bow of gratitude to the panel participants: Cooper Lee Bombardier, Ryka Aoki, Colette Arrand, Brook Shelley, and Grace Reynolds for their inspiration.

My mosaic, created in the "cut-up" style the panel emulated, draws on the following texts:

- Jan Morris, *Conundrum* (New York Review Books Classics, 2006)
- Jennifer Finney Boylan, *She's Not There: A Life in Two Genders* (Crown Reprint, 2103)
- Arin Andrews, *Some Assembly Required* (Simon and Schuster Books for Young Readers; Reprint Edition, 2015)
- Andrea Long Chu, *My New Vagina Won't Make Me Happy* (New York Times, November 24, 2018)
- Jamison Green, *Becoming a Visible Man* (Vanderbilt University Press, 2004)
- Rae Spoon and Ivan E. Coyote, *Gender Failure* (Arsenal Pulp Press, 2014)
- Cameron Awkward-Rich, *Sympathetic Little Monsters* (Ricochet Editions, 2016)
- Jordy Rosenberg, *Confessions of the Fox* (One World, 2018)
- Cooper Lee Bombardier, *Pass With Care* (Dottir Press, 2020)
- Thomas Page McBee, *Man Alive* (City Lights Publishers, 2014)

homecoming was a literary theme as old as Homer's *Odyssey*. But what I saw in you and what I read in trans memoirs was a story of homecoming with a strange and imaginative twist. Whereas Odysseus gazed out the window of Calypso's castle and recalled his beloved Ithaca, you followed an impulse toward an imagined home, one you sensed in the core of yourself, but had not experienced when you told me you thought you would feel more at home in a boy's body. In my eyes you, and your trans community, were accomplishing an enormous feat of the human spirit, charting a course home in which your only real map has been the whisper of intuition, and your only real vehicle the strength of your imagination.

REFLECTION QUESTIONS

- In Oklahoma our family learned about an Indigenous approach to health that considered wellness from the perspective of mental health, physical health, spiritual health, and community health. What would spiritual wellness look like for your child and your family?
- What meaning is emerging from your family's gender journey?
- Does your child experience a sense of destiny, creativity, or agency in social transformation?
- How is your family's community health?
- Does your child feel a strong sense of belonging? If not, where might you look for environments that

would be a good fit for your child? Is there a camp or a conference or a support group that might help you find a community?

- Do you have a sense of belonging with your fellow parents? What could you do to seek company and companionship in your experience in your family's gender journey?

Letter 21

February 2020: Taking the Plunge

For President's Day weekend, we planned a boys' trip to Disneyland with Atticus, your seven-year-old cousin who had never been. The last time you had visited, you were in elementary school, near the time we had started working with Leslie, and you had chosen to skip many of the rides. At that age, you craved big movements with your body, but only if you controlled them. You shied away from intense inputs that came from the world around you. This time, though, you were amped up about the rides. You wanted Space Mountain and the Incredicoaster, Mr. Toad's Wild Ride and Splash Mountain. Amusement parks had never been my thing, and as the trip approached, I held on to a tiny stash of dread, and I knew how that little bit of dread could gather momentum. I could already hear myself telling the group I'd "go get some Cokes," instead of fully experiencing Disneyland. No one would have batted an eye, but it was not what I wanted. You were just on the cusp of your 14th birthday; it had come up so fast and you had come so far in your relationship to your body and your senses. I didn't want to miss a minute of the joy. So, before we left, I made you promise to not let me duck out of any rides.

What I did not realize was that Melinda your aunt, was crazy for Disneyland. Normally quiet and reserved, she emerged as a veritable theme park drill sergeant. She and Uncle Mark had arrived with Atticus a few hours before us, and they had already ridden the Incredicoaster twice. I couldn't believe that he had ridden the loop-de-loop, upside-down roller coaster, and when I asked him how it was, he shrugged ambivalently and said, "Pretty good. A little scary at first, but it was okay the second time." I looked at my brother wide-eyed. We had grown up in a house where our preferences and fears had been respected, maybe even coddled. It was hard to imagine my brother taking a seven-year-old on an upside-down roller coaster. He laughed and said, "Don't look at me," and pointed to Melinda.

When Mark had tried to prepare Atticus for that first ride, getting down on his knee to talk to him at his level about what to expect, Melinda had interrupted. "Don't do *that*. It'll scare him. It's a ride. He'll be fine." And that's how they had ridden the Incredicoaster twice already. If Atticus could survive Melinda's program, I figured I could too. We'd be fine—my new mantra for the park.

Melinda had visited Disneyland many years in a row as part of her high school marching band. Our trip was her first time back in many, many years, and she had a carefully laid-out plan for how to get to as many rides as possible over the few days we were there. It started with the Incredicoaster. No warming up, no Ten Thousand Leagues Under the Sea or It's a Small World. According to Melinda's way, the opening ride needed to get your adrenaline pumping. In line for the Incredicoaster, my little stash of dread swelled to as big as your camp duffel while we waited. I had never ridden a roller coaster that looped upside down. My hands started to sweat; my throat closed a little. My stomach felt like it was zooming down the drops before we even boarded. I tried to reframe the sensations as excitement, but I didn't buy my own manipulation of the facts. Instead, I reminded myself the ride couldn't be longer than a few minutes. We'd be fine.

You and I took seats next to each other. I stuffed my purse in the tight mesh pocket, and when the shoulder bars clicked down on us, I reached for your hand and closed my eyes. The car swooped out of the loading dock and picked up speed. I felt us climb and drop and bank side to side. We screamed when we sluiced into weightlessness. When we flew through the loop-de-loop, I laughed as hard as I had in years. The smooth curl upside down had spun my insides like a somersault. I recognized the sensation. It was new but not new, a cousin to the same weightless spiral that I liked to repeat in my pool as a girl.

Stepping out of the car, we were breathless. Our little family team cackled and preened. We high-fived and recounted every twist and turn. You were elated. You wanted to do it again. You looked over Melinda's shoulder at the map; where was Thunder Mountain, where was Splash Mountain, where was Space Mountain? We had to do them all.

By the end of the trip, we had done them all, plus the Incredicoaster three times. We fiercely debated whether Splash Mountain or Guardians of the Galaxy (a ride I had grown up knowing as Tower of Terror) was the best. You loved the photographs we bought of us careening down Splash Mountain, and dreamed of returning to Disney to stage a photo like the season pass holders did; maybe you'd pull out a perfect chessboard or an inflatable giraffe so that it could be immortalized on camera. I calculated when we could return, and in the back of my mind planned to bring you back with a friend after you finished the school year and graduated eighth grade.

Although not much had changed in the world around us—Trump was still president, your fertility options were experimental, our country and town were still home to people who hated trans people—I left Disneyland feeling like we had tossed fear off our shoulders. That little stash of dread had grown huge waiting online before every new, scary ride, and then emptied out when it was through. One ride at a time, we both left a little bit of fear behind. It was one more way we were learning to push past our comfort zones and be brave. It was good (and fun!) training for our gender journey that was pushing us in so many new ways. I was not surprised that shortly after we arrived home you told me you had been thinking and you wanted to go for it. You wanted to try the egg retrieval.

Letter 22
March 2020: Stuck

We had briefly considered extracting an ovary instead of doing an egg retrieval cycle. The idea of one short surgical procedure had an appeal in comparison to the two weeks of shots, repetitive blood draws, and physical exams. But Dr. Kim had convinced us that the technology for future egg fertilization was far better understood than the alternative. If we had decided to extract tissue, we would have been betting that the technology for growing eggs from ovarian tissue would develop while you were growing up, whereas IVF technology was already firmly established. So the plan was set. You would stay on your blockers, take a series of hormone shots that would grow egg follicles from your prepubescent oocytes, and then Dr. Kim would retrieve the ones that matured to freeze them for your future. Essentially, we would be suspending reproductive material in time until you were ready to make your own choices about biological parenting. All while preventing your pituitary and other glands from kicking off puberty in the rest of your body.

The earliest we could begin the cycle was the end of March, a month after your 14th birthday, which meant you'd need to delay your first testosterone shot. In the years since you had first visited the gender clinic, that first shot seemed to live in your mind like the summit of Everest. How many times had I seen you look at yourself in the mirror like you were looking at a stranger? It wasn't just that you disliked your looks; it was almost as if they startled you because they looked like they belonged to someone else—your round baby cheeks, your narrow shoulders, and your undefined chest. Your chest especially had given you trouble, the way its subtle contours seemed to constantly threaten a turn toward femininity. I had always curbed the pain of your dysphoria with the promise that we were doing everything we could to get your body on the right path. I reminded you that those "T" shots were coming, which always gave you a sense of relief. Deciding to push that first shot out by a month must have felt like reaching a false peak on the trail; just when you thought you were about to summit, you saw another long stretch ahead.

By the time your 14th birthday came, Covid-19 had already been in the news for a few weeks. It was still being discussed as something far away that we mostly assumed was happening in China. I considered cancelling your birthday party. After Disneyland, you wanted to do something high energy with a couple of friends, so we had planned to take a small group of you to ride go-carts around an indoor track. We decided to go ahead with the party and took you and your friends to eat bad pizza and zip around an indoor course for an hour. A week later, Governor Newsom declared California's state-wide shelter in place. I'm glad we stayed safe and still got to have your party. There was no way of knowing how long of a stretch of isolation we were in for.

There was a disorientation to the early weeks of the pandemic that reminded me of your middle years. During both eras, our family's usual reference points disappeared, and we lived in an in-between time that was outside of what felt steady and predictable. Most of the time when you were young, I had trained myself to focus on the positive side, to see the possibilities when I dropped assumptions about your gender. But at the beginning of the pandemic, forgotten waves of sadness washed over me without warning. I recalled the times I cried in the car, at the gym, in line in the grocery store. I was not sleeping again, which reminded me of the many nights I lost to worrying about you. When you were young, so many people suggested that I was grieving the child they imagined I lost when your gender identity became clearer. But that was never how it felt to me, and being misunderstood about my experience contributed to my sadness. When I followed the thread of my feelings, they always led me to outer influences over which we had so little control—other people's attitudes, problems of technology, political disagreement in which trans lives were being pushed around like pawns on a chessboard.

During the early pandemic, I also felt a particular sadness for the way we lost the comforting containment of language. Both while your gender was in flux and during early shelter in place, there were words that lost their meaning and that loss of meaning dislocated us.

When middle gender became our description for your gender presentation, we struggled to find a word for who you had become to your sisters. "Sibling" was the obvious choice, but sibling felt clinical, a word used to describe the outcome of a Punnett Square genetics problem. "Sister" or "brother" felt as familiar as the front door to our home. The hinged syllables swung open, then slammed shut, just like an old screen door. Sister or brother implied shared family experiences—long afternoons of tag and hide-n-seek, endless hours squeezed into the back seat of a car, elbowing each other or trying to ignore the elbowing, generation after generation of relatives commiserating over the pains and oddities of life with shared parents. You and your sisters shared the same relationship that I shared with my brother, but during the years our family lived outside the binary concept of gender, language no longer held our family together in the same way. It made me feel disoriented, sometimes even panicked. The linguistic and cognitive isolation had been profound.

Aspects of shelter in place felt similar to me. Important words were suddenly stripped of meaning. "School" was a word that became a digital husk of itself. It was supposed to smell like pencil shavings and feel like a cool desktop after recess. It was supposed to sound like friendly banter and the voice of a teacher telling you to quiet down. But it transformed into something else altogether. The buildings still existed, and the group of students still gathered online. But your shared place—Lizzie's fourth grade classroom always came to mind when this thought came up, that room that was painted teal, that had cubbies marked with each student's name and desks set up in groups of four—had become a new kind of purgatory.

Brother, sister, school, I knew these words were more than just words. They were landmarks that located us and informed us of who we were in relation to the world and to each other. When those landmarks changed or collapsed during the in-between times, we felt expelled from our familiar lives. And in a real sense we were—we had been forced outside the bounds of what had been normal for us—both during your middle years and during the pandemic. You had worked so hard to climb into the firm hold of the language and gender identity that was right for you, and then the pandemic pushed you back into limbo.

During shelter in place, time felt like a river behind a dam. It accumulated without moving forward at all. A week into shelter in place, your appointments to begin your egg retrieval cycle were cancelled indefinitely. How long could you stand holding back the current of your life?

So much changed at once. Like everyone else, we moved every aspect of our lives into our home. I stopped going to the store. I stockpiled rice, beans, flour, and sugar. I froze four pounds of chicken thighs. Hoarding toilet paper seemed like uncivilized madness to me, so I didn't, and ended up regretting the choice. Among the caravan of logistical changes in the house, a few weeks passed by before we really talked about what your cancelled appointments meant to you.

The pandemic, generally, had you glum. The erratic, hard-to-follow Zoom schedule. The separation from your friends. The way everyday felt like the same day over and over and over again. It was hard to tell how much of your mood had to do with being stuck in the house and how much had to do with being stuck in a pre-testosterone time zone. The lack of control over either sapped you of the vigor that had been so present in Disneyland. When you finally asked me in a quiet moment what was going to happen with your appointments and I said I didn't know, you looked wilted like a plant that needed water. You wanted to know when I thought we would get news, and I didn't know anything about that either.

I looked into your eyes then and told you that you didn't have to do the retrieval. That when the world opened up again, whenever that would be, you could go ahead and start the testosterone that had already, in the best-case scenario, been postponed by a month. I didn't know exactly what pressure was building inside of you, but I heard it when you talked to me about how tall your friends were getting, who had started shaving, whose voice was cracking on the Zoom calls. As your mother, it had felt important to me to find the best options for you that I could, but as time began to accumulate, I felt more and more strongly that what I wanted for you was not a future baby but the opportunity for your adult self to have some choice in how to build a family.

It had been important for me to fight for you to have this option. And in the new quiet corners of time that opened up in the cancellation of all of our out-of-the-house activities, I saw how I had advocated for you the way I had wanted to be advocated for as a young woman. I had become the parent I had wanted during those years that my parents' marriage was falling apart. When I went looking for a new school for you, I was pushing back on that Harvard dean who had dismissed my ambitions. When I left clinicians who I felt weren't listening to you or to me, I was demanding more listening from my parents, requesting that they stay on top of their bills, requiring that they help me move my brother out of school. And when I went to the Supreme Court, I was telling the young woman I was that the world she had inherited had not been designed for her, that difficulty balancing parenting and meaningful work was built into the equation, and that despite the unfair calculus, the world needed her to be present, watchful, and engaged. I had fought for you, but I had also fought on behalf of the young woman I had been all those years ago. When the pandemic arrived, the time was ripe for the next steps of your journey to wholly belong to you. You had matured enough to understand the stakes of fertility loss and enough to know how much more waiting you could handle mentally and physically. I was not going to stop supporting you, but I had been pushing hard for so long; I wanted you to know that the process really belonged to you.

You didn't know right then what you wanted to do. You said it would depend on how long we ended up having to wait.

Letter 23
June 2020: Retrieval

Dr. Kim's office started to see patients again in late May of 2020. You learned that you could complete your retrieval cycle and start testosterone before leaving for summer camp, which had become your quiet goal. When you reunited with your camp friends, if you reunited with your camp friends, you wanted to be one of the guys who was on "T" already. It struck me as good judgment on your part, because it would allow you to administer your shots independently, but with a little bit of scaffolding by adults other than Dad and me.

Waiting this long represented a significant delay for you, and when I asked you how you handled it, you told me two things. First, you had waited so long already. The more time went by, the more effort it represented, and the less you wanted to blow up your plan. You knew there was a limit to how long this thinking would last and by May, your ability to wait was abating. And then you told me the second thing. When you felt tired of waiting, you thought of all the other trans kids who had it harder than you did. All the trans kids whose parents didn't support them, whose insurance didn't cover the blockers, whose communities and teachers and ministers were rejecting them. Your wisdom impressed me more than I probably said.

During one of your early appointments at the IVF clinic, Dr. Kim had told us she thought you would be the fourth trans boy in the country to retrieve eggs without experiencing an estrogen puberty. Standing outside the elevator you asked me, "So if I do this, will it help other people?" and I explained that you and the other trans boys who were the first to do these retrievals would make up a cohort who had the opportunity to prove it was possible for trans men who transitioned early to raise their own babies. Knowing that it mattered to others gave you motivation, and while you waited all those long months, you leaned into this awareness.

We started the hormone cycle in mid-June, and while it was logistically burdensome to time the shots and drive back and forth to the city for blood work and ultrasounds, it was less difficult than either of us anticipated, but still a little awkward. The evening of your first shot I had set up a mini pharmacy in the guest room bathroom. At the prescribed time we closed ourselves behind the door. You sat on the edge of the toilet and I stood holding a syringe. Then you said something that will make me laugh for the rest of my life: "Mom, I'd feel a lot more comfortable if a real doctor were doing my shots." The truth was, I felt the same way, and the thought of puncturing your skin with the syringe turned my stomach. But I put my mom-face on and chirped, "Don't worry. We'll be fine." My mantra from Disneyland.

The morning of your egg retrieval, we waited for your procedure in the most beautiful exam room I'd ever been in. Through floor-to-ceiling windows looking out over San Francisco Bay, we watched a group of small sailboats chase one another across the water. Wind filled the white sails, and sunlight glinted off the corrugated surface of the bay like handfuls of tossed coins. The clean light pouring into the room highlighted the steel IV stand and the polished floor beneath us. A nurse named Andrea who had candy-colored tattoos and gold sunburst earplugs made sure you had warm blankets and joked with us to put you at ease. When she asked you to disrobe completely under the gown, you tugged at my sleeve to ask if I would ask her if you could wait to get completely undressed. Nurse Andrea agreed that you could wait until you were ready.

Outside the boats zipped around in what looked like a game of tag until they seemed to slow almost to a stop. Then one by one they capsized. The tips of sails kissed the water then plunged below as hulls rolled their long keels toward the sun. A sailing class. I had been in one like it myself when I was your age. And even though I knew the sailors below us were practicing a drill, I still thought of the frigid bay water, the heavy winds, and the weight of soaked clothes hanging off of freezing hands and legs. I remembered how my own heart had pounded as the boat had turned over. Even in a drill, the elements of crisis—vulnerable lungs, the strong forces of wind, and the overwhelming weight of water—were present.

From the sixth floor of that beautiful all-glass building, we watched tiny sailors right their boats one by one. I recalled my own capsized sailboat from so long ago. The way the boat required what seemed like more than my whole weight to sway back toward the open sky. In the midst of the effort, righting the boat seemed impossible, until suddenly momentum shifted, and the return upright felt inevitable.

When Nurse Andrea told you it was time for you to leave me

and walk with her to your procedure, I put the white surgical shower cap on your head. I tied your gown closed behind you. By then, she understood the particular burden of nakedness for you, and rather than let the surgical gown flap around, she brought you another warm blanket to throw over your shoulders to protect your privacy. You squeezed your fingers against the rims of your eyes. "I don't know why I'm crying," you said. I looked into your eyes, cupping your face in my hands and said, "It's okay to cry." For a minute, you buried your face into my shoulder, and I held you. You took a deep breath and stood up tall. Then we took a step apart from each other. I held you by both shoulders and said, "I love you. They'll take good care of you. You've got this." You gave a nod and stepped away from me following Nurse Andrea down a long hallway. From behind, the blanket that draped over your shoulders looked like a cape, and you looked like a hero who had accepted his fate.

I had envisioned this moment as if it were some kind of finish line. After years of being told that you needed to accept permanent infertility in order to live in harmony with your body, here you were, one of just a handful of trans boys proving otherwise. And yet, what was present as you headed toward the operating room was not the thrill of outrunning a limit, but the rawness of the fact that there were limits at all. That we were made of flesh, separate bodies, destined to face our own fragility alone. It was a lesson your life was teaching you so young.

When I met you in the recovery room, you were in a different mood than when you left me. Your anesthesia had not worn off and you were busy praising everything and everyone. "Dr. Kim was amazing." "My nurse was amazing." Then you told me the apple juice they gave you was the best you ever had.

"It went well, didn't it, Dr. Kim? It was a big success, right?" you asked.

"Yes, Jake. Yes, it was," she said, still in her scrubs, her surgical cap on her head. Then she turned to me, "We retrieved 14 follicles. Over the weekend we will see which ones mature. We should be able to freeze a good number of them." It was excellent news. This really was the moment we had been waiting for. Later, when I shared your outcome with the founding endocrinologist at the UCSF pediatric gender clinic, he called your procedure "groundbreaking." But standing by your bed in the recovery room, I didn't feel it. I tried to imagine your follicles growing in their petri dishes, but I couldn't. I wanted to celebrate the moment, but the victory was abstract, and the pandemic had fogged up the usual clarity with which I experienced joy.

"You deserve a yummy lunch after fasting before the procedure," Dr. Kim said. "Have you planned what you're going to have?" You and I looked at each other and shrugged. You were drugged, and I was trying to get my bearings. We both love food, and it was unlike us to not have a plan about what to eat, especially when a celebration was called for.

"Do you like dumplings?"

"I love dumplings!" you cheered, your enthusiasm fueled by a genuine fondness for dumplings and a little by the drugs.

"Check out Dumpling Time. I think you can order online and then pick up. They are not far from here. I sometimes bring them home for my family for special occasions."

She left the room, and I looked up the Dumpling Time menu on my phone.

"What do you think? Soup dumplings?" I asked.

"Yes! I love soup dumplings!?"

"How about bao buns?"

"Yup!?" And gyoza and siu mai and sweet bao. We ordered them all. Driving home, our car windows steamed up from the heat thrown off by so many dumplings. When we arrived and I spread them out on the counter, all those warm dough bundles cradled in their take-out boxes, I felt some of the joy we had earned. Dad and I had discovered an opportunity for you, and you had taken it. In the wake of your choosing, some miraculous abundance had arrived. You had produced 14 follicles. Dr. Kim called me a few days later to tell me that seven of the eggs looked very healthy and had been frozen successfully. They will be waiting for your future self at her lab in San Francisco if you ever choose to build a biological family of your own.

REFLECTION QUESTIONS

- Parenting and family life can be demanding. Gender journeys can also be demanding. If you took on the mantra, "Celebrate every win, no matter how small," what would you celebrate today? This week? This month?
- What rituals draw your family? Do you like to bake? Decorate? Go out for milkshakes? Toast with silly glasses? How can you use rituals of celebration that already exist in your family to bond and lighten up your life as it relates to gender? What new rituals or rites could you invent that would give you and your family a boost or a sense of accomplishment?

Letter 24

June 2020: Exit Ticket

Completion comes in its own time, when it comes at all. Sometimes we set our sights on goals that end up being secondary to the growth we needed to experience on our way to them. Perhaps this was the reason retrieving your eggs had not been accompanied by the clear feeling of victory I had expected. We had learned that living in a trans body, during the early twenty-first century, was bound to be an iterative process. Transition and family building, like gender itself, would be an ongoing negotiation between nature, nurture, and culture, none of which would remain static. Egg retrieval was not an end point, but the beginning of an entire new narrative, suspended in time, waiting for a future that was impossible to envision.

A few days before your retrieval, the Supreme Court had delivered its decision in Aimee Stephens' case. It was a 6–3 victory in favor of Aimee Stephens and the trans community. Chief Justice Roberts, who had fumbled through the vocabulary, and Justice Gorsuch, one of Trump's appointees, voted with the progressive Justices of the Court. The decision secured discrimination protections for the trans community across the country, and it stood as a strong rebuke against the pointed policies and executive orders that Trump's administration had put in place against the trans community. A future in which our entire country had become safer for you had been secured. It was an unexpected and more decisive victory than anyone, even the attorneys who had argued the case, had been able to envision.

Aimee Stephens died before the decision had been delivered, which felt tragic. But I took comfort in the fact that when I had seen her speak in the fall, she had said that, for her, the journey itself was the victory. When she had been fired from her job all those years ago, she never imagined the impact her story would have or the community that would rise up to support her. Claiming her identity, fighting on behalf of her community, and receiving the support that her courage mobilized—these were her personal triumphs. And still, her case is a lasting artifact of her life, and it will improve countless trans lives in the future. To celebrate her bravery and her victory, I bought a cake. When it was time for dessert, I handed you the knife to slice into it for us. I wanted you to be the first to see the rainbow layers hiding inside the white frosting.

From your perspective it was fun to have cake, but your rights in a state like Oklahoma, and the notion of a Supreme Court case, were abstract compared to your pandemic life. And the success of the court case, although it did make you feel safer, didn't transform your relationship to the world around you the way your eighth grade graduation did.

The graduation was nothing like any of us had been conditioned to expect. There was no great hall with proud parents and grandparents. No diplomas handed out on a raised stage. No photographs with friends. No chorus of sentimental songs. Everything had been moved online. Your diploma had been mailed to our home, and the ceremony took place in our dining room. When your name was called, our family's gallery square on Zoom launched into the speaker position as Dad and I handed you the dark blue folio with your name printed across the top.

Later in the morning, you invited us to a separate online event that your school called your "Exit Ticket." Every student led a presentation that represented their middle school journey. During your talk Dad and I sat behind you, so we saw you from the back, while you presented into your computer screen.

You walked the group through a comic strip that you had drawn of a ronin and his dragon. In the opening frame, the ronin was learning how to use his weapons. He had some successes in fights, but a few frames into the story he was confronted by a dragon that was beyond his abilities. The ronin was forced to retreat and practice his skills for a long time. As you described the various skills the ronin was practicing, you shared the various aspects of your experience that had been meaningful to you in middle school, your favorite projects, the teachers who supported your learning, the challenge of learning the science behind CRISPR genetic engineering, which had been some of the most difficult and satisfying material for you to master. As the comic strip frames proceeded, the ronin's skills became stronger and more precise. Until the dragon returned.

Now a masterful fighter, the ronin entered the final few frames prepared with his sword. But when he encountered the dragon close up, he realized the dragon wasn't an enemy at all, but a powerful being he needed to befriend. Instead of fighting against the dragon, he practiced with the dragon, inventing new strategies they could deploy together as a team to vanquish their shared enemies. The final frame was a beautiful sketch, the lines of the ronin and the dragon were confident and dynamic, expressing new stability and strength. Your teachers and friends on the Zoom call cheered for the ronin and the dragon. We all thought your talk was over.

But then you paused, and your voice hitched the tiniest bit. You quieted down your cheering online audience. "Guys, guys. I'm not done yet," you said. You thanked everyone for their friendship and told them how intimidating it had been to join a new school in the seventh grade. You talked about all the people who had helped make that transition easy and fun. Then you described how much trust you felt for your school community, and that, because of that trust, you wanted to share something important with them. "I'm trans. My name used to be Jane. And I just want you all to know how much your friendship and support these last two years has meant to me." All around the Zoom gallery, adults started to cry. Your advisor Tom, your teacher Ben, Lisa who had arranged your first visit. While I pressed the wetness from my eyes, I tried to memorize the feeling in my body. From my waist down, I felt rooted to the earth, solid, like I could not be budged, and from my waist up I felt tall and warm like a sunflower that was turning toward bright afternoon light. You told the story of your personal triumph in such a way that it returned a portion of the victory back to the people who had been your friends. I was proud.

I believed then and I believe now that some part of you will always be that eighth-grade boy sharing his moment in the spotlight with his friends. Making everyone else believe they had helped make the beauty of your life possible. You were a boy in full possession of himself, giving and receiving in equal measure. I imagined the moment looping in an infinite spiral. Time felt strange to me right then. In the course of a year and a half, it had borne down on us, with its relentless, repeating beats forward, but I felt sure that it had somehow become limitless too. That it swirled and eddied in occasional collisions of past and future, forming tiny galaxies where love and spirit were as reliable and ubiquitous as gravity. Artifacts and images and dreams that came from us could slip out of the heavy stream and outlast us. In the face of our own fragility, we were also, in part, unbreakable.

In bed that night, I conjured my faithful scene. There you were at my bedside. Your hair cropped close to your neck; your bangs swished across your forehead. It was the haircut you had gotten the week before graduation. I realized you were going to keep the style for a long time. The square of your shoulders filled your shirtsleeves, and the small boy next to you held your hand. For the first time, you could speak to me. "Hi, Mom," you said. I smiled. My body felt the lift of a thousand light wings flying.

Who of me had died, I wondered.

The doubtful one, I answered.

Then I opened up my eyes.

It is always good to see you, son.

Afterword
Interview with Jake

Jake is my son, a 15-year-old boy who enjoys drawing, playing video games, and petting his cats. He is training for his black belt in taekwondo, and when he grows up he wants to draw graphic novels and spend some part of his life working as a fire fighter and first responder.

Cristina: Jake, it was a really big deal to let me write about your story. What made you feel supportive about the book and why do you want people to know about your life?

Jake: I think it's important for people to know that this is what the reality is or could be like. You always see these bad stories, but my story encompasses a realistic idea of a supportive parent. It's not gonna be perfect, because nothing's perfect, but there hasn't ever been a time where you told me "Oh, no, you can't dress like that," or "Oh, no, you can't do that." Whatever I felt like doing, I kind of just did. And that was the key to figuring out my identity. I feel like it's a lot more confusing if you're trying to fit into something instead of just letting the kid figure it out.

I always kind of saw myself as a tomboy. And then when I started to get to puberty I realized there was stuff that I wanted to change about myself. I remember whenever I was thinking about myself when I was older I would always think of myself as a dad. And then I would correct myself, "Oh, wait, no, I have to be like, a mom." I remember asking you, "How can you not get boobs when you grow up?" And then I remember when I first started using he/him pronouns: I was like, yeah, I like this. It was a lot more fitting. I thought about staying "middle," but when I used he/him pronouns and thought about the deep voice I felt like it would fit me better. I thought it would be awesome.

Cristina: Yes, that's the joy I've always seen in you. That's why I called the book *About Bliss*; whenever you've done something that's taken you more down the masculine spectrum, I have always seen your energy increase. Can we move to a new topic? Talk a little about what motivated you to do the egg retrieval?

Jake: It was about having options. I knew it was kind of gonna stink to do it. But I also knew if I grew up, and I realized I wanted my own kid, it would stink even more to know I had the option and I didn't take myself up on it. I thought it would be better to just have one hard week instead of a lifetime of "Dang, I really wish I could have my own kid." I'd be totally happy with adopting a kid. I just thought in the long run there could be some point where I'd want a biological kid.

And honestly, it wasn't that bad. I did it over a break, too. So it wasn't disruptive. In the moment it seemed kind of bad. And it was overwhelming to have all the female stuff, like getting a period. I really felt uncomfortable with that. But it was only a week. And then it was over. It was pretty easy.

Also, not many people have retrieved eggs without going off blockers. So I wanted to do it also for, not for science exactly, but just because it could be helping a lot of other people. I knew if I did it, and it ended up successful, then that would be pretty monumental for other people. I'm always keeping in mind that it might not work, obviously, because it's prepubertal. But if it does work...

Cristina: It's really brave to share your life with other people. What it's like for you to think about other people reading about you? Is there anything you want readers to know or to take from your story?

Jake: I think it is a little nerve-racking in the sense that it's always going to be out there. That's why I want to change my name in the story. Because, if it does get published, it's for the rest of my life. I just want to be seen as me. Not like he's trans and he has a story. If my story is introduced before, say, I go into a meeting and other people are talking to me as a trans person rather than just seeing my personality, it's a lot different. I'm totally fine with who I am, I just want to be seen as me first.

But I also really want other trans kids to know they can stay true to themselves. I think the best thing about my story is that I always just did my thing. And by doing my thing I really grew to feel confident in who I was. And I feel really strong about my identity. I know a lot of people go through a time of panic or distress, or wanting to act, like, hyper feminine if they were assigned female at birth, to convince themselves that they're not trans, but I just want people to know that being trans is a real thing. I especially want other people who are more conservative to read the book and really get it. Because there are a lot of negative opinions out there. I want people to realize being trans is just people being true to themselves.

Acknowledgments

Middle school is hard. Raising children is hard. Raising children with needs that fall outside the mainstream is very hard. Managing serious illness is hard. And writing a book is hard. On any given day, someone might ask me how I've done these things. On one level we are all doing our best to meet the requirements our lives present. We don't have a choice about our toughest assignments, so we put one foot in front of the other. This is simple, but many days, for many people, not so easy. What makes putting one foot in front of the other possible for me is keeping good company. Full stop. I've never believed in going it alone, and that's a fortunate mindset, because my life, and particularly my writing, would not be possible as a solo trek. I owe most of what is good, and certainly what is good about this book, to the warm hearts who support me, the beings I get to call family, friends, teachers, partners, caregivers, allies, and more. Some people say it takes a village; in the case of our family, it takes something more like a small country.

Creating a container of time and solitude is essential to thinking well, and for me, this was especially true when managing a long-form project. The only person who ever got in the way of me taking time for myself was me. Many times I was embarrassed to need the help that I did. I thought I should handle things alone; I felt guilty for spending money on the support that it turns out I needed. Eventually, I made the decision that one way I personally could smash the patriarchy was to be as clear-eyed as I could be about the labor associated with mothering and wifing/housekeeping. And I could allow myself to get support. This was harder than you might think. There were a lot of internal walls that I needed to take down.

Everyone else, especially my husband Graham, granted me generous permission to chase down my thinking. He encouraged me to invest our family resources in great people who have helped us raise our three kids and maintain a sane household. The labor that goes into these two endeavors—childrearing and housekeeping—is often unnamed, invisible, and undervalued. May this not be so when it comes to this project.

This book has been a team effort. Rosalba S. has put in long hours for over 20 years. She showers us with unearned affection and supports us with unwavering reliability and commitment. Amanda Martino, Shaunice Sili, and Jasmine Meuller-Hsia are all women wise beyond their years. Each of them brought unique gifts to our children, and introduced Graham and me to parenting strategies we would not have encountered otherwise. And Melissa Abel. She catches my spinning plates as they whirl off their sticks. I've never seen her miss. She is compassionate, detail-oriented, graceful, and fierce when necessary.

Two drafts before I completed this book, Graham was diagnosed with amyotrophic lateral sclerosis, more commonly known as ALS, or Lou Gehrig's disease, a devastating motor neuron disease that is 100 percent fatal. Within a year of his diagnosis (and before the book was complete) I needed substantial caregiving support just to get through the day. Because of the professionalism and care of this team, Graham has a high quality of life. He keeps us laughing, helps the kids with math, continues to think his big thoughts, and generally continues to be himself despite all that ALS has taken from him. To Aida, Josese, Dale, Dane, David, John, Roberto, Rex, Matthew, and Korina, our family is grateful beyond what words can express. May all families who need care encounter such warm, professional, trustworthy, and positive nurses and caregivers.

Parenting a gender-expansive child is a beautiful but complex affair. At every turn we have been supported by extraordinary gender-affirming practitioners. The clinicians at the Stanford Pediatric and Adolescent Gender Clinic and at the UCSF Child and Adolescent Gender Center are leaders in their field who work at the front lines to make sure gender-expansive kids get the care they need. Diane Ehrensaft's books are a guiding light for so many families. Diane's support for our family and for this book have been invaluable.

I might not have attempted writing a book if it had not been for Melanie Thernstrom, a mom I met when our kids were in preschool together. Melanie is a celebrated features writer for *The New York Times* and the author of three books. I stalked her a little bit, to be honest, and when I shyly admitted (or dropped the hint) that I wrote a little too, she generously offered to read my work. I can still hear her saying, "Of course you can write a book," which was a dream of mine, but at the time sounded completely outlandish. She thought maybe an MFA would be good for me.

Shortly after meeting Melanie I went to a writing retreat with Cheryl Strayed on Maui. There were about seventy of us there, writing and fangirling over Cheryl. When someone asked, "What do you think about getting an MFA?" Cheryl's response was, "It doesn't hurt. If you can do it without going into major debt, it doesn't hurt." The writers I met at that retreat became my MFA classmates, my writing partners, and some of the most trusted readers and collaborators in my writing life. Sheila Hamilton and Amy Lyons, I am so grateful we were on Maui at the same time.

I wrote the first draft of this book as an MFA student at Bennington College Writing Seminars, a low residency MFA program located in Vermont. Bennington and my teachers there made me a writer. My time in the program was one of the happiest times in my life, and I consider myself extremely lucky to have studied there. Each of my instructors improved my craft and encouraged me to keep going. To Susan Cheever, Sven Birkerts, Dinah Lenney, Peter Trachtenberg, Clifford Thompson, and Benjamin Anastas I offer a deep bow of thanks. You set a high bar that I will be trying to reach for the rest of my life. I never could have finished the book without extra support from Benjamin Anastas.

Through Sheila Hamilton, I connected with an incredible community of writers who have fed my writer's soul closer to home. On Sheila's recommendation I continued to expand my artistic learning at Corporeal Writing, a writing collaborative founded by Lidia Yuknavitch. Domi, Katie, Janice, Daniel, Domi, Leigh, and Lidia—my art is more alive because you have shared art-making space and practices with me. I am grateful to swim in your waters.

Through Sheila I also met other literary artists who have helped me along the way. Laura Stanfill and Laura Mazer both offered me wonderful advice along the way. And Liz Prato has become a friend, mentor, reader, and inspiration. It was through Liz that I met Alex DiFrancesco, who, through twists of fate, became the editor of this book. Our family's story could not have a better steward. Alex is the author of four books and also works as an editor. They have an artist's eye, an advocate's voice, and a shaman's heart. As a parent, writing about one's children presents several ethical issues, and these issues are multiplied when your family's history is sensitive. Alex understood the stakes from the beginning and has been a trustworthy partner in a kind of storytelling that I hope will plant seeds of peace and healing.

Wendy Levinson is the agent a debut writer needs. Her commitment to this book has been unwavering. She invested in me and my work down to the line level, so that when it was time to find my book a home, it was the very best it could be. She has been a smart and generous collaborator as we have strategized about how best to introduce editors to what was a controversial issue and has only become more so over time.

The process of placing a manuscript is the stuff of writers' deepest insecurities. Even when the work is good, there is always the chance that it won't connect. When I was experiencing the apex of these fears, Cindy DiTiberio (publisher of *Literary Mama* and author of *The Mother Lode* newsletter) swooped in and gave me important practical writing advice and support.

This project would not have been possible without the support of the trans thought leaders who agreed to contribute interviews to the book. Their wisdom is priceless, and it gives me a great deal of comfort to have such an amazing team of trans adults anchoring my family's story. In my mind, I see a circle of strong, healthy, protective adults standing sentry for my son. This fine group of people is there for him in ways he probably still does not understand. I am so grateful to Shawn Giammattei, Alex DiFrancesco, Chase Strangio, Kelley Blair, Shannon Minter, Andrew Hedges, and Nick Teich for their presence in this book and in my family's life. My son's life is possible because of his trans ancestors.

Friendship has always been an important value in my life, but in 2020, in the depths of the pandemic when Graham was diagnosed with ALS, my friends became my life raft. Brette Hudacek, Gina Parks, Kirsten Romer, Nancy Rosenthal, Deb Whitman, and Debbie Wolter, our circle holds me on the rim when I feel like I can't hold on. Laurel, from the minute you put your arms around me and said, "We'll get through this. We will," I knew we would. Alison, I carry your heart voice in mine. Clarissa, I'll skate with you anywhere. Katherine, averaging with you makes me a better, stronger, kinder person. Kirsti, thank you for seeing and supporting all of me. And to my physically far, but spiritually close, sisterfriends, Jennifer Amis, Valerie Brooks, Juliana Farrell, Kiersten Todt, and Jenifer Smyth, thank you for a lifetime of connection.

Our parents George and Linda, Philip and Bernice, my mom Katherine, and my Aunt Virginia have always been my most ardent fans. Graham and I both started our adult lives with the benefit of stellar educations that our parents made possible. They believe in us as people and as parents. We are lucky. A special shout out to my mom who has made a habit of telling me, "cream always rises to the top," when I have doubted myself.

When Graham and I married, I made him a small ceramic tile on which I painted the words "Spencer Family Artist Colony," heralding our creative future. I'm not sure either of us fully knew how literal this dream was for me. Enter our three children. Their early childhood years brought this dream to life and gave me license to conjure artistic space. I filled our home with silks and felts, markers and paint brushes. Costumes and cameras and rubber stamps. A sewing machine. Baskets of yarn. Instruments.

American adults, by and large, should not collect such impractical stuff. But raising my kids let loose a yearning. I made this space for them, but I also made it for me. It turned out to hold us all, even Graham, in a wholesome way. My children are my earliest collaborators. They are the people I most enjoy making good trouble with, and they are the artists I most enjoy tracking. Each has developed their own powerful creative lexicon, and having a front row seat to their creative unfolding has been one of the greatest pleasures of my life. Miss G, Kooks, Bun, thank you for sharing yourselves with me. To my son, who is offering the world so much by letting them into his childhood, you have been making the world a better place for a very long time.

My writing life would not exist without my husband Graham. His intelligence shines a kind of light most people don't ever get to see in their lifetime. People who know him well—friends, colleagues, and family—know what I mean when I say this. Experiencing myself and my work in his light has been the gift of a lifetime. His mind, his ambition, and his optimism have inspired so many people, but no one more than me. ALS has not diminished him but distilled his finest qualities. Graham, I am grateful for every day we have together. Thank you for everything.

Resources

Books

Memoirs by trans writers guided me at many points in our family's journey. The collection below highlights books that provide especially strong first-person accounts of gender dysphoria.

- Arin Andrews, *Some Assembly Required: The Not-So-Secret Life of a Transgender Teen* (Simon & Schuster Books for Young Readers; Reprint edition, 2015)
- S. Bear Bergman, *The Nearest Exit May Be Behind You* (Arsenal Pulp Press, 2009)
- S. Bear Bergman, *Special Topics in Being a Human: A Queer and Tender Guide to Things I've Learned the Hard Way about Caring for People, Including Myself* (Arsenal Pulp Press, 2021)
- Cooper Lee Bombardier, *Pass with Care* (Dottir Press, 2020)
- Kate Bornstein and S. Bear Bergman, *Gender Outlaws: The Next Generation* (Seal Press; Reprint edition, 2010)
- Jennifer Finney Boylan, *She's Not There: A Life in Two Genders* (Crown; Reprint edition, 2013)
- Alex DiFrancesco, *Psychopomps* (Civil Coping Mechanisms, 2019)

- Jamison Green, *Becoming a Visible Man* (Vanderbilt University Press; Second edition, 2020)
- Jack Halberstam, *Trans*: A Quick and Quirky Account of Gender Variability* (University of California Press, 2017)
- Thomas Page McBee, *Amateur: A True Story about What Makes a Man* (Scribner; Reprint edition, 2019)
- Thomas Page McBee, *Man Alive: A True Story of Violence, Forgiveness and Becoming a Man* (City Lights Publishers, 2014)
- Jan Morris, *Conundrum* (New York Review of Books Classics, 2006)
- Rae Spoon and Ivan E. Coyote, *Gender Failure* (Arsenal Pulp Press; Second Printing edition, 2014)

Fiction

This list includes adult and young adult fiction by trans and cis writers.

- Laurie Frankel, *This Is How It Always Is* (Flatiron, 2017)
- Alex Gino, *George* (Scholastic Press, 2015)
- Ami Polonsky, *Gracefully Grayson* (Little Brown Books for Young Readers, 2014)
- Jordy Rosenberg, *Confessions of the Fox* (One World, 2018)
- Ellen Wittlinger, *Parrotfish* (Simon & Schuster Books for Young Readers; Reissue edition, 2019)

Nonfiction guidebooks

- Michele Agnello, *Raising the Transgender Child* (Seal Press, 2016)
- Stephanie Brill and Lisa Kenney, *Transgender Teen: A Handbook*

for Parents and Professionals Supporting Transgender and Non-Binary Teens (Cleis Press, 2016)
- Stephanie Brill and Rachel Pepper, *The Transgender Child: A Handbook for Families and Professionals* (Cleis Press, 2008)
- Juno Dawson, *This Book is Gay* (Sourcebooks Fire, 2015)
- Diane Ehrensaft, *Gender Explained: A New Understanding of Gender in a Gender Creative World* (The Experiment, 2024)
- Diane Ehrensaft, *The Gender Creative Child: Pathways for Nurturing and Supporting Children Who Live Outside Gender Boxes* (The Experiment, 2016)
- Diane Ehrensaft, *Gender Born, Gender Made: Raising Healthy Gender-Nonconforming Children* (The Experiment; 3rd Revised edition, 2011)
- Laura Erickson-Schroth, *Trans Bodies Trans Selves: A Resource for the Transgender Community* (Oxford University Press, 2014)
- Mady G and Jules Zuckerberg, *A Quick & Easy Guide to Queer & Trans Identities* (Oni Press, 2019)

Organizations

- Free Mom Hugs, support and education for families, chapters in all fifty states: https://freemomhugs.org
- Gender Spectrum, workshops, support groups, and a national conference in the summer: www.genderspectrum.org
- GSLEN, national network of educators and students creating more affirming school environments: www.glsen.org
- Trans Families, support and education for families, organizers of the Gender Odyssey national conference: https://transfamilies.org
- Transgender Law Center, support for changing names and

gender markers on identification: https://transgenderlawcenter.org

- Trans Student Educational Resources, youth-led advocacy and support for trans youth: https://transstudent.org
- Trans Youth Equality Foundation, education, advocacy and support for trans youth and their families: www.transyouthequality.org
- The Trevor Project, advocacy, research, and crisis counseling for the LGBTQ+ community: www.thetrevorproject.org

Pediatric gender clinics

For a complete list of US pediatric gender centers, visit the Trans Health Project at Transgender Legal Defense & Education Fund (TLDEF): https://transhealthproject.org/resources/academic-gender-centers

- BOSTON, MA
  Gender Multispecialty Service (GeMS), Boston Children's Hospital: Tel: (617) 355-4367; www.childrenshospital.org/programs/gender-multispecialty-service

- CHICAGO, IL
  Gender Development Program and Lurie Children's, Children's Hospital of Chicago: Tel: (800) 543-7362; www.luriechildrens.org/en/specialties-conditions/gender-development-program

- CINCINNATI, OH
  Transgender Health Center, Cincinnati Children's: Tel: (513) 636-4681; www.cincinnatichildrens.org/service/t/transgender

- DENVER, CO
  TRUE Center for Gender Diversity, Children's Hospital Colorado: Tel: (720) 777-8783; www.childrenscolorado.org/doctors-and-departments/departments/gender-diversity-center

- DURHAM, NC
  Duke Child and Adolescent Gender Care Clinic, Duke Children's Health Center: Tel: (919) 684-8361; www.dukehealth.org/locations/duke-child-and-adolescent-gender-care-clinic

- HOUSTON, TX
  Gender Medicine Program, Texas Children's Hospital: Tel: (832) 822-3670; www.texaschildrens.org/departments/gender-medicine-program

- LOS ANGELES, CA
  The Center for Transyouth Health and Development, Children's Hospital Los Angeles: Tel: (323) 361-2153; www.chla.org/adolescent-and-young-adult-medicine/center-transyouth-health-and-development

- MINNEAPOLIS, MN
  Gender Health program, Children's Minnesota: Tel: (612) 813-7950; www.childrensmn.org/services/care-specialties-departments/gender-health

- NEW YORK, NY
  Gender & Sexuality Service, Children's Hospital at NYU Langone: Tel: (646) 754-4958; https://nyulangone.org/locations/child-study-center/gender-sexuality-service

- PHILADELPHIA, PA
  Gender and Sexuality Development Program, Children's Hospital of Philadelphia: Tel: (267) 426-5980; www.chop.edu/centers-programs/gender-and-sexuality-development-program

- SAN FRANCISCO, CA
  Child & Adolescent Gender Center: Tel: (415) 353-7337; www.ucsfbenioffchildrens.org/clinics/child-and-adolescent-gender-center

- WASHINGTON, DC
  Gender Development Program, Children's National: Tel: (202) 476-5744; www.childrensnational.org/get-care/departments/gender-development-program